The World of Biblical Israel

Cynthia R. Chapman, Th.D.

THE
GREAT
COURSES

PUBLISHED BY:

THE GREAT COURSES
Corporate Headquarters
4840 Westfields Boulevard, Suite 500
Chantilly, Virginia 20151-2299
Phone: 1-800-832-2412
Fax: 703-378-3819
www.thegreatcourses.com

Cynthia R. Chapman, Th.D.
Associate Professor of Biblical Studies
Oberlin College of Arts and Sciences

Cynthia R. Chapman is an Associate Professor of Biblical Studies at Oberlin College of Arts and Sciences in Oberlin, Ohio, where she has taught for 11 years. She holds a B.A. from Kalamazoo College, an M.Div. from Vanderbilt Divinity School, and a Th.D. from Harvard Divinity School. At Oberlin, she offers courses in both the Old and New Testaments. Among the courses she most enjoys teaching are The Nature of Suffering: The Book of Job and Its History of Interpretation; The Bible in the Christian Communities of Asia, Africa and Latin America; and Biblical Women in Text and Tradition.

Professor Chapman's research has focused on the historiography of the Bible considered within the larger ancient Near Eastern environment and on gender in ancient Israel. Her first book, entitled *The Gendered Language of Warfare in the Israelite-Assyrian Encounter*, explored the shared use of gendered literary tropes in the Bible and Assyrian royal texts as both Israel and Assyria claimed masculine victories for themselves while feminizing their enemies. Professor Chapman is currently completing her second book, entitled *The House of the Mother: The Social Function of Maternal Kin in Biblical Hebrew Narrative*. This book demonstrates that kinship bonds established through the mother served vital social and political functions for a son who aspired to inherit in his father's household. A chapter of this book that focuses on the kinship-forging properties of breast milk has been published in the online *Journal of Hebrew Scriptures* as an article entitled "'Oh that you were like a brother to me, one who had nursed at my mother's breasts.' Breast Milk as a Kinship-Forging Substance" (http://www.jhsonline.org/Articles/article_169.pdf). ∎

Table of Contents

Table of Contents

Table of Contents

The World of Biblical Israel

Scope:

Thishis course traces the history of biblical Israel from its origins in the central highland villages just west of the Jordan River (1200 B.C.E.) to its emergence as a nation, and, then, a pair of kingdoms. It examines the impact of political and military domination by the successive empires of Assyria and Babylonia that resulted in the disappearance of the northern kingdom of Israel and the exile of the southern kingdom of Judah to Babylonia. Historically, the course concludes with the return of the Judean exiles from Babylonia to Judah during the time of the Persian Empire (6th–5th centuries B.C.E.).

The lectures emphasize how the catastrophic experience of the Babylonian conquest of Jerusalem in 586 B.C.E. and the deportation of a large segment of the literate population of Judah to Babylonia served as the impetus for compiling, editing, and preserving scripture. As such, the Babylonian Exile informs our reading of the biblical text. Much of what we learn about life in biblical Israel is preserved in our Bible because it spoke to the needs and longings of a people who were living in exile. Because the Bible is written from a particular historical perspective, we will frequently turn to archaeological evidence to augment and often challenge the biblical picture of life in ancient Israel.

The course is divided into six historical units. The first unit introduces life in the Babylonian Exile, where conquered Judeans sought to maintain a sense of their national identity while living in a foreign land. It is within this exilic setting that Judeans sat together and told their children who were born in exile all the stories of life in their homeland in Israel. They told the family stories of Abraham and Sarah, Isaac and Rebekah, and Jacob and his twelve sons to communicate to their children the values and religious beliefs that they now considered central to their survival as a people. They also told their children the remarkable story of how their national deity had empowered an ancestor named Moses to lead the Hebrew slaves out of Egypt, across a desert wilderness, to the gateway of the Promised Land. These memories of an exiled people preserve authentic aspects of life in ancient Israel during its earliest periods while speaking to the needs of an exiled people who hoped they, too, would be delivered from bondage and led back to the Promised Land.

The second and third units cover the history of Israel from its origins as a nation in the land to its flourishing as two independent kingdoms: Israel and Judah (1200–745 B.C.E.). Within this historical framework, we examine the economic life of a rural highland family. We survey Israelite kinship structures and marriage practices and the development of political systems. We also explore the diversity that characterized ancient Israelite religious beliefs and practices, and finally, we consider what it meant to be rich and what it meant to be poor during the time of the monarchy.

In units four and five, we cover the life of Israelites and Judeans as they experienced imperial domination, conquest, and ultimately, exile under the Assyrians and Babylonians (745–538 B.C.E.). Within this time period, we examine the advanced military technology of Assyria and Babylonia, including the use of psychological warfare. We continue to trace developments within religious practices and beliefs that were clearly influenced by the encounters with powerful enemies from Mesopotamia. One of the most significant religious developments that emerged in the context of exile was the articulation of monotheism, the belief that the Israelite god was in fact the only living god, the creator of the cosmos. Finally, we study the role of literacy throughout Israel's history but with a specific emphasis on the period of the Babylonian Exile. It was during the exile that a group of literate scribes preserved a body of texts that ultimately preserved the people that gave the world the Bible.

Our final unit covers the period of Judah's resettlement in the land, where the people identify themselves as the "New Israel," restored to their homeland. The issues of life that became important during this period are those that involved preserving national identity. We will listen in on debates about intermarriage, national boundaries, and the importance of the family meal. Finally, we will close the course with two biblical stories of loss and restoration that encapsulate the history of life in biblical Israel while offering multiple interpretations of what that history means. These are the stories of Abraham's near sacrifice and loss of his son Isaac, who is then restored to him by an angel's command to spare the child, and the story of Job's shattering loss of wealth, family, and personal health and, then, for reasons that are still debated today, his full restoration. Both of these stories spoke powerfully to a people who had lost land, family, temple, and seemingly, their god but found themselves miraculously restored to their homeland with a chance to rebuild. ■

Biblical Israel—The Story of a People
Lecture 1

Biblical Israel is a land and a people that in many ways seem familiar to us. We know what the "Holy Land" is today: a place that three of the world's religions consider sacred. Many of us can immediately bring to mind pictures of modern Jerusalem, with the ancient walled city in its midst. But when we turn to the Israel described in the Bible, we have to use imagination. What might this land have looked like in 1200 B.C.E., when a people called the Israelites first appeared on the terraced hillsides of a land called Canaan? In this course, we'll use biblical stories and archaeological artifacts to give us a window into life in this ancient time.

The Bible as a Source
- Without question, the Bible is a tremendously valuable library or ancient archive. In it, we find ancient Israel's favorite stories, official and popular histories, poems, prayers, and laws. The Bible is also a place where we can eavesdrop on ancient political and religious debates.

- Although the Bible is a valuable archive of historical materials, it is not objective or comprehensive. It was not written as an ethnography. Instead, ancient Israelites preserved particular stories, laws, and histories because they considered them worth passing down to the next generation. Many of the stories focus on heroes, extraordinary men and women who had miraculous encounters with the Israelite god.

- The story of Elijah, a biblical hero from the books of 1 and 2 Kings, illustrates how the Bible can help us learn what life was like in ancient Israel.
  - Elijah was an Israelite prophet, and several events in his life have a legendary, miraculous quality. For example, he does not die but is taken up into heaven in a chariot of fire. Elijah is anything but a "typical ancient Israelite," and these miraculous

occurrences suggest that his story will not be helpful in uncovering the lives of ancient Israelites.

o But then we read of his encounter with a woman called the widow of Zarephath (1 Kings 17:8–24). Elijah goes to Zarephath, a town on the northern coast of Phoenicia, because God has told him that in the midst of a famine, he has commanded a widow there to feed the prophet. Miraculously, the widow's food supply does not run out for the duration of the famine. Later, the widow's son falls mortally ill, but Elijah revives the child.

o On the surface, this is yet another story of Elijah as a miracle worker. It serves the theological purpose of calling on Israelites to serve the one living God, who can work miracles and sustain life. But in the midst of these miracles, the story inadvertently relates several details about the everyday life of a poor widow, each of which finds repeated confirmation in the archaeological record of ancient Israel.

• As we continue to turn to the Bible as a source for life in biblical Israel, we will look for these small details and everyday encounters that help us imagine what life was like in this ancient land.

Defining "Israel"
• When we talk about ancient Israel, we tend to think of it as a fixed entity, something that is clearly defined in terms of geography and culture.

Elijah revives the son of the widow of Zarephath by calling on the name of his god.

But the definition of "Israel" changes with each historical period we will study in this course.

- On a map, we find ancient Israel located near the Mediterranean coast on the western side of the Fertile Crescent. A journey through this region would begin at the Euphrates River, travel north to modern Turkey and across the ancient Hittite and Hurrian kingdoms, shift south near Aram and Damascus in modern Syria, and end in the land of Canaan, where Israel first emerged as a people and a nation around 1200 B.C.E. At this earliest stage, Israel was located in the central highlands, just west of the Jordan River.
  - Several biblical journeys are charted along the Fertile Crescent, including that of Abraham, the founding ancestor of the Israelite people.

  - The major powers in the region included Egypt in the southwest, Mesopotamia in the east, and the Hittite kingdom in the north.

- The geographic region from Syria to the southern desert bordering Egypt is called the Levant; in this region, we find several minor powers surrounding Israel, including Edom, Moab, and Ammon, located just across the Jordan River; Philistia, along the Mediterranean coast; Aram and Phoenicia to the north; and the Canaanite city-states in the central plains.

- The main history that is narrated in the Bible begins about 1400 B.C.E. and extends through around 400 B.C.E., from Israel's remembered origins in its founding ancestors through its emergence as a people and a kingdom. It continues by recording Israel's and, later, Judah's experiences of conquest and deportation at the hands of Assyria and then Babylonia and, finally, to its rebuilding as a nation during the Persian Empire.

- The meaning of the word "Israel" shifts over time in the Bible to refer to a person, a nation, a united monarchy, a divided monarchy, a remnant, and the restored Israel.
  - The story of Jacob wrestling with an angel is our first encounter with the word "Israel" in the Bible (Gen. 32:24–32), where it clearly refers to a person. (The biblical chronology of Israel starts here, c. 1400 B.C.E.) The angel says to Jacob: "Your name shall no more be called Jacob but Israel, for you have striven with God and with men and have prevailed."

  - The patriarch Jacob had twelve sons, whose descendants became the "nation of Israel" in the books of Joshua and Judges (c. 1200 B.C.E.).

  - In the book of 1 Samuel, "Israel" is the name of a united monarchy headed by King David and his son Solomon. Here, "Israel" designates a kingdom made up of twelve tribes (c. 1000–950 B.C.E.).

  - After only 75 years, the united monarchy is divided (1–2 Kings). A rebellion within the twelve tribes results in a schism, and "Israel" becomes the designation for the ten northern tribes; "Judah" is the designation for the single tribe in the south. "Israel" during this time of the divided monarchy is still a kingdom, but it is a smaller kingdom (950–586 B.C.E.).

○ The northern kingdom of Israel falls to Assyria in 722 B.C.E., and the southern kingdom of Judah falls to Babylonia in 586 B.C.E. Judah alone continues to exist as a people in exile. As the sole remnant of the original twelve tribes of Israel (722, 586–538 B.C.E.), Judah becomes the memory holder for Israel. By surviving as a people, Judah wins the right to tell the story of Israel, and in that story, Judah sees itself as the "remnant of Israel."

○ On their return to their homeland (beginning in 538 to c. 400 B.C.E.), the exiles from Babylonia brought with them a book, some form of the Torah. In it, they had preserved the story and the memory of their eponymous ancestor, Jacob. These returning exiles saw themselves as the New Israel and the House of Jacob. Like their ancestor, they felt that in exile, they also had wrestled with their god and had come away both permanently marked and blessed.

• In every period described in the Bible, Israel is of central importance. It is the chosen person, nation, kingdom, and remnant of the Israelite god.

Archaeology of Israel
• Fortunately, in our examination of the history and daily life of ancient Israel, the Bible is not our only source. Archaeology of the land of ancient Israel and the surrounding ancient Near East has proven enormously helpful in coming to a better understanding of what life was like for average people. In addition to artifacts related to daily living, archaeological excavation has also yielded royal texts that provide an outsider's view of Israel.

• When we turn to other nations' views of Israel and uses of the term "Israel," we get a different picture from that presented in the Bible.

- The first extra-biblical reference to Israel is found on an Egyptian victory stele of Pharaoh Merneptah, dating to around 1200 B.C.E. "Israel" on this stele is a group of people in the land of Canaan, but it is not a chosen people of God. It is one among several peoples and cities that Merneptah celebrates conquering.

- A second extra-biblical reference to Israel is found on the Black Obelisk of the Assyrian king Shalmaneser III. This monument records the tribute received from several conquered regions, including Israel.

- What "Israel" signifies depends on the time period and the source document. In the Bible itself, Israel represents a remembered history and a present reality; a person, a people, a monarchy, and a hope. In nonbiblical sources, Israel is listed among several other nations that the much larger countries of Egypt and Assyria had conquered.

Chosenness

- One consistent feature across time and nation is that in every written record we have, each country sees its own history as divinely guided and its own military victories as divinely secured. Each country had its own national deity or set of deities.

- In English translations of the Bible, we find the Israelite national deity referred to as either "God" or "the Lord," while the gods of other nations are referred to with personal names, such as Dagon or Chemosh. These two labels used for the Israelite god, God and Lord, reflect two different Hebrew ways of referring to this national deity
  - In several texts, the Israelite god is referred to with the Hebrew word *elohim*, which is a generic word for "god" or "gods" but is clearly used as a kind of proper name for the Israelite god in the biblical text.

9

- o In many other texts, the Israelite god is referred to as Yahweh, which is his personal name. Because this name was considered too holy to pronounce by those who recorded the written biblical text, only its consonants were preserved: YHWH.

- o The English translation that replaces the personal name of the Israelite god with the epithet "Lord" reflects a centuries-old tradition of not pronouncing Yahweh.

- This course focuses on a time when Israel and all the surrounding nations each had a national deity with a name. To accurately reflect this period, we will use the terms "Israelite god," "Israelite national deity," and "Yahweh," to come to a better understanding of the religious landscape of ancient Israel, rather than the religious landscape reflected in our English Bible translations.

- We can see the importance of this terminology when we realize that each nation during the period of biblical history saw itself to be in some way chosen by its own national deity.

Suggested Reading

Coogan, *The Old Testament*, pp. 22–32.

Smith, *The Memoirs of God*, pp. 7–45.

Questions to Consider

1. In what ways can the Bible provide us with historically valuable information about ancient Israel?

2. What do we learn about Israel from the royal victory monuments of foreign nations that claim to have conquered Israel?

3. Why is the name of the Israelite god important for understanding the ancient Israelite nation and its people?

4. How does the idea of "chosenness" affect the historical portrait of Israel preserved in the Bible?

By the Rivers of Babylon—Exile
Lecture 2

In our last lecture, we discussed the Bible as a resource for our study of life in ancient Israel. In a sense, the ancient Israelites left us their library; perusing the shelves helps us discover who they were and why they collected this set of books. But if we're going to use the Bible as an ancient library, we need to take a moment to understand who produced it and when. What happened in the lives of ancient Israelites that caused them, unlike any of their neighbors, to preserve their history in writing and successfully pass that history down to succeeding generations? We'll explore that question in this lecture, the first in a unit on stories of origin.

The Babylonian Exile

- Psalm 137 describes the period known as the Babylonian Exile, which began in 597 but is most commonly dated to 586 B.C.E., when Babylonia conquered Jerusalem and Judah and deported many of the inhabitants.

  o It was after this national defeat and crisis that many of the books of the Bible were compiled, edited, and shaped into a library.

  o The selection of stories seems designed to respond in some way to the realities of being an exiled people.

- The Bible describes the actual event of the conquest in a surprisingly brief text in 2 Kings 25:8–12.

  o During the reign of King Zedekiah of Judah, Nebuchadrezzar, the king of Babylon, came to Jerusalem and "burned the house of the Lord, and the king's house and all the houses of Jerusalem; … he broke down the walls around Jerusalem." Aside from a group described as the "poorest of the land," all the people— "the rest of the multitude"—were carried into exile.

- o Why did a military defeat and a national displacement serve as a catalyst for the collection and editing of a nation's history? Periods of national crisis are often followed by a reshaping of a nation's story, as we see in our own history with such events as the Vietnam War or 9/11.

- Although the Bible does not give us a great deal of detail concerning the individual experiences of deported Judeans, we can make some generalizations based on what we know to be the military practices of Babylonia in this period. Judeans at all levels of society may well have been forced to watch as their family members were killed, as was the case with King Zedekiah. They would have seen their homes burned and their sacred sites looted.

- Tens of thousands of Judeans were probably taken into exile. They would have traveled from Jerusalem north into Syria, east across southern Turkey, and finally, south along the Euphrates River into what was then Babylonia (modern Iraq), a distance of 800 to 900 miles. Because the group included women, children, and the elderly, the journey would have been long and slow, and it's likely that many people died along the way.

- Once the Judean exiles arrived in Babylonia, a new stage of transition would begin. They would find themselves in a land very different from their own, surrounded by a people who spoke a foreign language and worshipped foreign gods.

- Much of what was ultimately preserved in the Bible speaks in some way to the horrific loss and displacement the Judeans experienced during the period of exile.

Psalm 137
- Psalm 137 was probably written during the Babylonian Exile and offers one of the few descriptions we have of exilic life.

- In the psalm, the captives ask, "How can we sing the Lord's song in a foreign land?" They have a sense that singing praises to their national deity requires being physically present in his temple or, at least, in their homeland. A god was tied to a land.

- In verses 5 and 6, the references to the right hand withering and the tongue cleaving to the roof of the mouth relate to singing and harp playing. If the captives forget Jerusalem, they will never sing or play the harp again.

© Getty Images/Photos.com/Thinkstock.

Psalm 137 gives us the context of exile—within which the Bible began to take shape as a historical narrative, a sacred memory, and ultimately a canon of scripture.

- In verse 7, there is a sharp shift in the language of the psalm from nostalgia and lament to anger and a call for revenge. The Judeans specifically call for revenge against the Edomites, who had rejoiced in Jerusalem's fall, and Babylon, the "devastator."

- Both parts of the psalm emphasize memory. The Judeans call on themselves to remember their homeland and capital city. Here, memory is infused with nostalgic longing and a conviction to endure. They also call on their god to remember who wronged them. This memory is infused with anger and a desire for revenge.

Lamentations 1
- Lamentations is a book of poetry that laments the conquest of Jerusalem by the Babylonians. It is different from Psalm 137 because it is set in the conquered city of Jerusalem rather than in exile.

- Verses 1–3a of Lamentations 1 give us a vision of a destroyed city and its inhabitants. Jerusalem has become a widow, a princess reduced to a vassal.

- In verse 7 of this chapter, we see again a reference to remembering: "Jerusalem remembers in the days of her affliction and wandering, all the precious things that were hers in the days of old."

Exile as the Context for Scriptural Formation

- Why did a military conquest and deportation cause the Judeans to record and preserve their history in writing and pass it down from generation to generation?

- First and foremost, the Bible tells a story, one that's organized into a simple chronology.
  - The story starts "in the beginning" with the creation of the world; it moves forward in time to the appearance of Israel as a family under the patriarch Jacob, who is renamed Israel. Then, we have the emergence of Israel as a nation of twelve tribes united, who conquer the Promised Land of Canaan. We move forward in time to the establishment of Israel as a kingdom, its conquest and deportation, and finally, the resettlement of the land.

  - This same history, however, could be told paying special attention to the contexts within which individual stories were written, compiled, edited, and retold. In this case, the exilic experience becomes a filter for which national stories are preserved and how they are presented. The crisis of exile posed questions. And the Judeans worked through those questions in part by recording their history, the history of who they had been when they were in their land.

- Psalm 137's question, "How can we sing the Lord's song in a foreign land?" is really a way of asking: How can we pass on or preserve a sense of identity in our children while we are in a foreign land? The context of exile posed questions, and it is possible to view the Bible as an effort to formulate answers to some of these exilic questions.

- If we examine the Bible in this way, the neat, linear timeline is replaced by a messier kind of diagram. But this messier version is likely much better for understanding what life was like in ancient Israel.

"Timeline" of Biblical Text Development

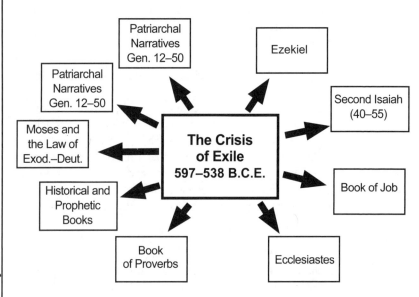

o In the center of the diagram is the exilic period, beginning in 597 and lasting until around 538, when some Judean exiles began returning to their homeland.

o In this period, Judeans began to reach back into their past to make sense of their present situation. Our diagram shows arrows going backward in time, representing an effort to retrieve and preserve history in order to retell it for children born in exile.

o   Not all of biblical history was written during the exile; rather, the context of the exile determined which histories to preserve and how to present them. Some of the scribal activity that began in exile involved gathering, sorting, and shaping existing written materials.

Questions Raised by Exile

- One question generated by living in exile that could be answered by retrieving and reshaping existing histories was this: How did Judeans fit in the foreign world to which they had been exiled?

  o   The first 11 chapters of Genesis, known as the "primeval history," provide a genealogy that traces humanity's ancestry back to a single couple, Adam and Eve, and its division into three distinct peoples under Noah's three sons.

  o   It is in these chapters that we find the creation story and learn that at the beginning of time, it was the Israelite god, not any of the Babylonian deities, who created the cosmos, formed the human creatures, and ultimately, organized the known world.

- The rest of the book of Genesis seems to address the question: Who are the Judeans as a people?

  o   Known as the "patriarchal narratives," the chapters of Genesis 12–50 assert that the Judeans are the heirs to a covenant that was promised to Abraham, Isaac, and Jacob.

  o   On the one hand, the story of the patriarchs remembers a time long past, when the ancestors of the Judeans first arrived in the land. On the other hand, the emphasis on an everlasting covenant and a gift of the land as an "everlasting possession" takes on new meaning to a people exiled outside their land.

  o   The books of Exodus, Leviticus, Numbers, and Deuteronomy narrate the history of the Judeans as a treasured possession of the Israelite god. They had lived in exile before and were rescued by their god and delivered to the Promised Land. The

Judeans are the covenantal partners of the Israelite god; if they keep his laws, he will be their god and protect them.

- The historical books of the Bible, together with the writings of the prophets, seem designed in part to answer the question: Why were the Judeans conquered? The most popular answer provided is that the Judeans were conquered not because the Israelite god was not strong enough to protect them, but because they had not fulfilled their side of the covenant.

- The book of Proverbs, structured as the advice of a father to a son, lists the values the Judeans should pass on to their children, including fear of, or reverence for, the Israelite god as the beginning of knowledge.

- In such books as Ezekiel, Isaiah, Ecclesiastes, and Job, we find the Judeans struggling with questions that could not be answered with existing histories and writings: Why are we being punished for the sins of our parents and grandparents against the covenant? What if our god is not just, not accessible, or not knowable? Has our god forgotten us?

- The story in the Bible is not written as objective history. Rather, it is the recorded memory of a conquered and exiled people determined to remember their past and pass that memory down from generation to generation.

Suggested Reading

Carr, *An Introduction to the Old Testament*, pp. 1–52.

Fleming, *The Legacy of Israel in Judah's Bible*, pp. xi–xv, 3–35.

Questions to Consider

1. Can you think of additional stories in the Bible that would speak to the crisis of exile?

2. How have national crises in the history of America reshaped our national narrative?

3. How does the role of memory or remembering help us to understand the kind of history that is preserved in the Bible?

Ancestor Narratives in Genesis
Lecture 3

As we saw in the last lecture, the recording of their "family stories" played an essential role in the survival of the Judeans during their exile in Babylonia. Ancient Israel understood itself to be a family that had descended from an ancestor named Jacob, whose name was ultimately changed by God to Israel. In our next two lectures, we will explore these stories, which are found in the first five books of the Bible and known collectively as the Torah. In this lecture, we'll look at the ancestor stories found in the book of Genesis, and in the next lecture, we'll turn to the story of Moses, who dominates the other four books of the Torah.

Authorship and Dating

- Traditionally, the authorship of the Torah has been attributed to Moses. But modern biblical scholarship ascribes the books to multiple authors and dates them to multiple periods. The earliest writings date centuries before the exile, and the latest compositions date to the 2nd century B.C.E., long after the exile.

- Scholars have come up with numerous ways to conceptualize the complexity of the biblical text, in this case, just the Torah.
  - Understanding the Torah as a tell (a mound formed by layers of human settlement) emphasizes the multiple layers of editing that generations have added to the foundational stories.

  - Thinking of the Torah as a curated artifact points to its enduring legacy and emphasizes its status as sacred scripture.

  - Thinking of the Torah as Israel's family heirloom leads us to the Babylonian Exile as a point of generational transfer, a time when one part of that family—the Judeans—made decisions about which of their stories to preserve and how to tell them.

- By the time the Judean exiles returned to their land after about three generations in Babylonia, the Torah had become a treasured story of origins passed down from generation to generation.
  - It had also become authoritative scripture, a story that priests read aloud at the temple during high holidays.

  - The process that led to these national family stories becoming scripture is murky. But it's clear that the experience of conquest and exile played a defining role because the stories that are preserved in the Torah speak powerfully to a landless people longing for their god to deliver them home.

Narrative Arc of the Torah
- The Torah narrates a history of about 3,000 years, from the creation of the universe to the arrival of the Israelites at the banks of the Jordan River, where they prepare to cross and take the Promised Land of Canaan.
  - Within this story, certain periods of history are rushed, condensed into a few chapters. Other periods are treated in enormous detail. This change in the pacing of the story shows which periods of history and which stories carried the most cultural weight.

  - The story of Moses dominates four of the five books in the Torah, and within that story, the episode of Moses receiving the law from God on Mount Sinai is the centerpiece. Second to Moses in emphasis is the family story of Abraham, Isaac, and Jacob. This ancestral history occupies most of the book of Genesis.

- In Genesis 12, the Israelite god, for reasons that are not stated, chooses one man, Abram (renamed Abraham), to bless in a special way. He asks Abraham to leave his homeland in Mesopotamia and move to the Promised Land in Canaan, where he would become "a great nation" blessed by this god.

- o The Israelite god repeatedly reveals himself to Abraham and to his descendants, Isaac and Jacob, and forms a covenant relationship with them.

- o God asks Abraham to "walk before me and be righteous." In return, Abraham receives God's promise that he will be the father of a "multitude of nations," and he is granted an eternal landholding in Canaan. As a mark of the covenant, Abraham is asked to circumcise himself and his male descendants.

- The rest of the book of Genesis narrates the history of Abraham, Isaac, Jacob, and Joseph—four generations. We often refer to the first three men as the "patriarchs."
  - o Each one experiences divine visitations, during which the terms of the Abrahamic covenant are reiterated.

  - o At the same time, each of these men faces serious challenges that seem to make the promises of land, progeny, blessings, and great nations useless. Abraham, for example, must wait 25 years from the time that he is first told he will father a great nation to the birth of the son that God has promised him. The patriarchs also face threats to their lives, often coming from God himself.

- Several of the recurring themes of the patriarchal narratives speak to the exilic reality of those preserving these stories.
  - o These themes include the Israelite god's presence and power, which transcend national boundaries; the covenantal relationship between Abraham's descendants and the Israelite god; the eternal nature of the covenantal relationship; and the gift of the Promised Land as an everlasting bequest.

  - o The stories also acknowledge tensions experienced by the exiles: wives who cannot conceive, children whose lives are threatened, a land prone to famine and war, and a god who does not always protect.

- Central to almost every aspect of the patriarchal stories is the blessing of children, a blessing that cannot be taken for granted at any period in ancient Israel's history. To an exilic community that had lost many children through war and sickness, stories of children who are born into a land inheritance would speak powerfully.

Jacob, the Father of Israel

- Like the exiles, Jacob lived most of his adult life in Mesopotamia, exiled from his family. While in exile, Jacob put down roots; he married four women and fathered twelve sons and a daughter. Among Jacob's twelve sons was a man named Judah, the tribal ancestor of those in exile.
  - Ancient Israel understood itself through the language of a family and organized the world into a family tree.

  - The story of Jacob's family provides the basis for how ancient Israel came to understand itself socially and politically as an alliance of twelve tribes.

- Jacob and his twin, Esau, were born to Isaac and Rebekah after a period of barrenness. The two are rivals from the womb. Throughout the childhood and early adulthood of these men, Jacob proves himself to be a clever and unscrupulous climber, who supplants his older brother as heir. He tricks the witless Esau out of his birthright and, with his mother's help, tricks his father, Isaac, into giving him the blessing of the firstborn that was meant for Esau.

- Because of the family strife between the twins, Jacob is ultimately forced to flee his brother and travel to Haran in Mesopotamia, where he finds refuge with his mother's brother Laban. While there, Jacob marries both of Laban's daughters, first Leah, the elder, and then Rachel, the younger.
  - Rachel is the beautiful and the loved wife, and Leah has "weak eyes" and is the unloved wife. But Leah is abundantly fertile while Rachel is barren. The ancient Israelite understanding

of fertility sees God as the one who opens and closes wombs, allowing or preventing conception.

o   This scenario of a dual marriage plays out in a kind of birthing war that ensues between the rival sisters. First, Leah gives birth to four sons. Rachel offers her maidservant, Bilhah, as a wife to Jacob, and Bilhah bears two more sons. Leah then offers her maidservant, Zilpah, to Jacob; she bears two sons. Leah bears two more sons and a daughter. Finally, Rachel gives birth to two sons.

o   In this way, the house of Jacob is made up of two primary wives and two secondary maidservant wives. Each wife seeks to secure and even elevate her status in her husband's house by bearing children.

•   The sons born to these four women are not regarded equally, not in the family story and not in the national story that grows out of this family. Firstborn sons stood to inherit a double portion from their father's estate. In Jacob's house, his firstborn son is Reuben, but it is Joseph, the firstborn of Rachel, who inherits the covenantal promises of Abraham, Isaac, and Jacob.

•   When Jacob ultimately returns home to Canaan, it is under the guidance and at the call of the Israelite god.
    o   Before reaching Canaan, Jacob camps on the eastern side of the river Jordan, spending a night alone. It is here that he wrestles with a mysterious "man" and is renamed "Israel."

    o   The identity of the midnight wrestler remains obscure. He refuses to give his name to Jacob, and although he is referred to as a man, Jacob ultimately concludes that he had wrestled with none other than God. He names the place of this encounter Peniel, meaning "face of God," because he says, "I have seen God face to face, and yet my life is preserved."

Jacob experiences a divine threat to his life when he wrestles with God throughout a night, barely surviving.

- Thus, the process through which Jacob becomes "Israel" is a long and arduous one. It has involved fleeing, exile, and hard labor. It has also involved fulfilling one of the patriarchal promises as he "becomes a great nation" through the birth of his twelve sons.

- Now that he is "Israel," he crosses the river Jordan, returning to the land of Canaan, the place where he has been promised a perpetual landholding.

- From the perspective of a people exiled from their land, living in Mesopotamia, the story of Jacob would be a powerful one of redemption.
  - The tribe of Judah, which ends up in exile in Babylonia, will likewise endure hard labor. They will take wives and build families, replenishing themselves into something resembling

"a great nation." Many will also build wealth in the land to which they are exiled.

o   And when they return to the land of Judah during the Persian period, they return not as Judah but as all Israel. They, too, are renamed before crossing the river Jordan back into the Promised Land.

Suggested Reading

Hendel, *Remembering Abraham*, pp. 3–56.

Levenson, *The Death and Resurrection of the Beloved Son*, pp. 55–68.

Questions to Consider

1. How does a genealogy function as a form of social and political organization?

2. When you read the stories of Genesis and keep in mind the exile as the context within which they were preserved and edited, what new details emerge as significant?

Moses—The Torah's Central Hero
Lecture 4

In the story of Moses, who spent his life in Egypt, we see a repetition of the pattern established with the patriarchs of living outside the Promised Land. Still, we sense geographic movement in Moses's story, from the rescue of the enslaved Israelites in Egypt, to the crossing of the desert wilderness, to the arrival on the banks of the Jordan River. Once again, we must imagine the exiled Judeans telling this story to their children and preserving it in writing. The story of Moses and the divine rescue of an enslaved people would not only build a sense of identity among the exiles, but it would also generate hope for a restored community in the Promised Land.

The Call of Moses

- The closing chapters of Genesis and the opening chapters of Exodus bridge the Torah's two stories of origins—the story of the ancestors and the story of Moses—genealogically and religiously.

- The story of Joseph, the son of Jacob, locates Joseph in Egypt, where he rises to a position of power in Pharaoh's court.
    - During a time of famine, Joseph's family resettles in Egypt, where Joseph secures their survival through distributing grain from Pharaoh's storehouses. Genesis ends with the death of Joseph and his deathbed promise to his brothers: "God will visit you, and bring you up out of this land to the land which he swore to Abraham, to Isaac, and to Jacob" (Gen. 50:24).

    - The book of Exodus opens with the descendants of the house of Jacob being fruitful to the point that "the land was filled with them." And a pharaoh arises in Egypt "who does not know Joseph"; out of fear of this numerous people, the pharaoh enslaves them.

- o In this manner, the descendants of Jacob are linked genealogically to a group called "the Hebrews," who are enslaved in Egypt.

- Exodus 3 gives us the story of the call of Moses. Here, the Israelite god appears to Moses in a burning bush.
  - o The god of the burning bush identifies himself in a way that directly connects him to the stories of the ancestors found in Genesis: "I am the god of your father, the god of Abraham, the god of Isaac, and the god of Jacob" (Exod. 3:6).

  - o He calls on Moses to announce to Pharaoh that he will bring the Israelite people out of slavery in Egypt and into the Promised Land of their fathers.

  - o After much resistance, Moses agrees, but he wants to know this god's name. The god of the burning bush answers, "I am who I am." When Moses then goes to the Hebrew slaves and tells them the name of the god who sent him, he switches the name to the third person, saying, "'He is who he is' sent me." It is from this third-person form of the sentence that we get the personal name of the Israelite god, Yahweh.

- What follows is the story of the Exodus and the receiving of the law on Mount Sinai; these two events are also the story of the birth of the nation of Israel.
  - o At the beginning of Exodus, the protagonists are Hebrew slaves oppressed by an Egyptian pharaoh. Then, the Israelite god rescues them. He brings them to Mount Sinai and binds them to himself in a covenant.

  - o By the end of the Torah, these Hebrew slaves have emerged as the nation of Israel, poised to enter a land promised to their ancestors. All this occurs under the divinely appointed leader, Moses.

The Exodus
- After the call from the burning bush, Moses goes to Pharaoh to demand the release of his people, the Hebrew slaves.
  - When Pharaoh refuses, God sends ten plagues. The final plague, the killing of the firstborn in every household in Egypt, causes Pharaoh to relent.

  - But he no sooner lets the Hebrews go then he decides to pursue them. In this pursuit, the Israelite god divides the Reed Sea (known biblically as the "Red Sea"), allowing the Hebrews to cross on dry land. When they reach the other side, the waters return, drowning Pharaoh's pursuing army.

- This deliverance from slavery is referred to biblically as "the Exodus." We have no extra-biblical sources that confirm the historicity of this story, in spite of having rather detailed historical records from the courts of Egyptian pharaohs.

- What we can say, however, is that the story of the Exodus was part of ancient Israel's cultural memory from its earliest recorded history. Long before the exile, the story of the Exodus was being passed down from generation to generation.

Giving of the Law at Sinai
- After escaping Egypt, Moses leads the people of Israel to the dwelling place of the Israelite god, Mount Sinai, where he hears the words of a new covenant (Exod. 19:4–6).

- In several ways, this covenant is similar to the Abrahamic covenant, but it also reveals some obvious differences.
  - The covenant starts with God listing what he has already done on behalf of the Israelite people. It then moves to what God now requires of the Israelites: that they obey his voice and his teachings. If they do so, they will become God's special possession.

o   In the Mosaic covenant, the requirements on the Israelite side are more clearly defined than they are in the Abrahamic covenant. In fact, when Moses returns to Mount Sinai with all the people waiting at the base of the mountain, he receives the Ten Commandments— the stipulations for maintaining this covenantal relationship with the Israelite god.

© iStockphoto/Thinkstock.

The Mosaic covenant is clear: Those who want to be the special possession of this god who has just delivered the Israelites from slavery in Egypt must keep his commandments.

Torah as "Law"

*   What follows the story of Sinai is a listing or compilation of numerous types of laws, all of which are now understood to be part of the covenantal stipulations outlined in the Mosaic covenant from Sinai.

o   It's clear from the content of the laws that many of them date to a period when the people were already living in the land of Israel. Others date even later, to the time of the Babylonian Exile.

o   Attributing all of Israel's laws to Moses on Mount Sinai is a way to imbue them with the authority of Moses and God.

o   Some of the laws are wonderful from a modern reader's perspective simply because they show that ancient people fought over the same things that we do, such as property boundaries and animal control.

- Some of the laws that sound quite different from our own—and, therefore, point to something more distinctly Israelite—are those that are based on the notion of holiness.
  - The word "holy" means to be "set apart." If Israel is to be a "holy nation," a "kingdom of priests," it must be set apart from other nations.

  - The laws of the Mosaic covenant explain how the Israelites are to set themselves apart. There should be no intermarriage, no worshipping of foreign gods, and no sharing of a common diet. The Israelites will also keep holy by observing sacred times.

  - Many of these laws that are attributed to Moses on Mount Sinai actually had the greatest social currency during and after exile. Beginning in exile, in the absence of their temple, their land, and their king, Judeans began to see the observance of the Sabbath, the keeping of kosher food regulations, and the importance of refraining from intermarriage as key components of their national identity.

Moses and the Origins of the Priesthood

- According to Moses's genealogy, he and his brother Aaron and sister Miriam are descendants of Levi, the third son of Leah. Although Moses is clearly the leading figure of the Torah, several stories suggest the later importance and authority of Aaron.

- In the later history of the nation of Israel, Levi, as a tribe, is associated with the priesthood, and Moses and Aaron become the eponymous ancestors of two rival priestly lines.
  - Those who descend from Moses are called the Levites; they function as priests in shrines throughout Israel and Judah and in a subordinate priestly role in the Jerusalem temple.

  - Those who descend from Aaron are simply called priests, but they are most closely associated with the Jerusalem temple, where their sacred functions and status are higher than those of the Levites.

- One of the places we find an origin story for this priestly rivalry between Moses and Aaron is in the golden calf incident in Exodus 32.
  - o Aaron tries to defend his actions in forming the calf, but he is clearly portrayed as the guilty party. The long-suffering righteousness of Moses is contrasted with the sinfulness of Aaron as a way of forecasting what will be an ongoing priestly rivalry.

  - o The golden calf comes to symbolize the epitome of evil and disobedience. And Moses's act of convincing his god to reduce the punishment of his people becomes the model for prophetic intercession.

The Torah's Stopping Point: The Plains of Moab
- Almost the entire book of Deuteronomy is set in a single place, the plains of Moab, overlooking the Promised Land. The book is written as a kind of last will and testament of Moses.

- Knowing that he will not enter the Promised Land, Moses retells his story from the time of the Exodus through this point at the gateway to the Promised Land.

- Moses reiterates the stipulations of the Mosaic covenant, but Deuteronomy adds to the conditional nature of this covenant with a series of blessings and curses.

Recurrent Themes
- The Torah as an origin story has several recurrent themes, including the chosen status of the Israelite people. Israel and its god are covenant partners; by virtue of this covenant, Israel is a kingdom of priests and a holy nation. Further, although much of the Torah focuses on the gift of the Promised Land to the Israelites, its stories consistently place the Israelites outside of the Promised Land.

- Returning to the captive Judeans on the banks of the rivers of Babylon, we can see why this exiled people would want to preserve these stories.

- The stories speak to the exilic reality of living outside of one's homeland and to the religious experience of needing to access one's god in a foreign land.

- They speak to the Israelite god's ability to step in and rescue his people from foreign oppressors.

- Perhaps most importantly, the stories of the Torah teach that adhering to the stipulations of the covenant is the best path forward for the exiles, a way to continue to exist as a covenantal people of the Israelite god.

Suggested Reading

Carr, *An Introduction to The Old Testament*, pp. 187–206.

Niditch, *Oral World and Written Word*.

Questions to Consider

1. Why do you think that so many stories in the Torah focus on ancestors who lived most of their lives outside of the land?

2. Why would an exiled community preserve extensive collections of laws that govern life and worship in the land of Israel and Judah?

3. Does the story of Moses read as history or legend?

4. How might these stories of origin contribute to the survival of Judah as a people in exile?

Becoming the Nation of Israel
Lecture 5

The biblical books seem to be organized chronologically. The stories of the Torah are set in the Late Bronze Age (1550–1200 B.C.E.), and the stories of Joshua and Judges move forward to Iron Age I (1200–1000 B.C.E.) However, these stories apply historically to more than one period. Thus, in this unit, as we examine the emergence of Israel as a nation, we will find that Genesis continues to be a helpful source text. As we move forward historically, all the books of the Torah continue to be relevant because even though they describe a period in the Late Bronze Age, they were written in light of a history that extends into the Babylonian Exile.

The Emergence of Israel as a Nation

- Historically, the year 1200 marks the shift between the Bronze Age and the Iron Age. A series of events defines this transition; these events become significant factors for our understanding of the beginnings of ancient Israel.

- The key event that marks the end of the Bronze Age is the collapse of the Canaanite city-states.
    - During the Late Bronze Age, Canaanite city-states headed by kings controlled the Levant and developed sophisticated systems of trade, communication, and agriculture. Egypt was the superpower that endeavored to control these Canaanite city-states.

    - At the end of the Bronze Age, for reasons that remain unclear, this system of city-states collapsed, and large numbers of people moved out of these regional centers. Although Egypt did not disappear, its power and influence in the region weakened during this time.

- A second event that occurred at the shift between the Bronze and Iron Ages in Canaan was the arrival of a new people, the Philistines.

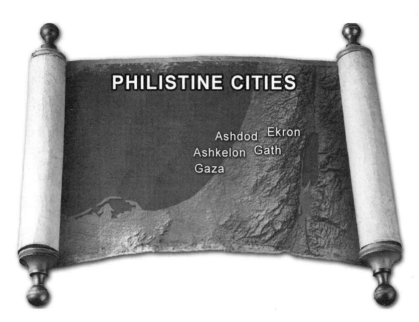

PHILISTINE CITIES

Ashdod Ekron
Ashkelon Gath
Gaza

This group arrived by sea to the southern Mediterranean coast of Canaan and settled in five cities. The Bible remembers these people as outsiders to the region, but it also recognizes them as fierce military competitors for the land of Canaan, a people who fought with weapons made of iron.

- Also dating to this historical moment of transformation between the Bronze Age and Iron Age is the Merneptah Stele that we saw earlier. Dating to around 1200 B.C.E., this Egyptian victory stele mentions "Israel" as a people in the land of Canaan that Pharaoh Merneptah conquered.

Occupation of Canaan in the Bible
- The Bible presents two versions of the story of how Israel came to occupy the land of Canaan. The first version, in the book of Joshua, presents the emergence of ancient Israel in the land of Canaan in a spectacular, if somewhat disturbing, conquest narrative.
  - o The book begins by signaling that Joshua has succeeded Moses as the divinely appointed leader of the twelve tribes

of Israel. Joshua gathers the twelve tribes so that they can cross the Jordan River and conquer the Promised Land of Canaan together.

o After crossing the Jordan River, Joshua accomplishes a rapid succession of astounding military victories that span the landmass of Canaan. These victories follow a pattern: They are divinely granted; they are fought together by all twelve tribes; and they involve "the ban" (Hebrew: *herem*), that is, the command given by God that the Israelites should "devote to the Lord the city and all that is within it for destruction" (Josh. 6:17).

o Once Joshua and "all Israel" had achieved a full military victory over the land of Canaan, God divided the Promised Land, giving each of the twelve tribes its own allotment.

o The book closes with a covenant renewal ceremony, in which the twelve tribes gather and swear loyalty to the Israelite god that granted them victory over their land.

• The book of Judges at first appears to be a continuation of the Joshua story, but it quickly becomes apparent that Judges is a second version of how and why ancient Israel emerged as a nation in the land of Canaan.

o The picture we get from Judges is one of gradual settlement of the tribes in various territories and through various means. Some conquered their territories; some made treaties and coexisted; some enslaved but did not kill the local populations. The process did not involve all twelve tribes working together.

o This situation of individual tribes or small groups of tribes cooperating to defend their territories seemed to endure for a couple centuries, known in biblical terms as the "period of the Judges" (1200–1000 B.C.E.).

- One characteristic example of the loose affiliation of tribes during this period is found in the Song of Deborah in Judges 5. The song celebrates the victory of the Israelites over the Canaanites of the northern city of Hazor. It calls for blessings on a group that is described as "the people (and commanders) who offered themselves willingly" (Judg. 5:2, 9) to this cause. In the end, we learn that victory was achieved by a coalition of six tribes.

- Much like the story of Elijah and the widow of Zarephath, the Song of Deborah clearly partakes of legend, but it also seems to preserve some important aspects of the historical period of Israel's emergence as a nation. It describes a loosely affiliated group of tribes that gather together under the leadership of the Israelite god and an appointed judge. They cooperate with one another insofar as their own interests are at stake.

- A comparison of the picture of Judges to that presented in Joshua reveals pronounced differences.
  - The structure of the book of Judges as a whole speaks to a different reality than the one described in Joshua. In Joshua, victory over the land of Canaan is achieved in one mighty military campaign. In Judges, we have a literary pattern that describes a period of peace under the leadership of a divinely designated judge, followed by a period of being conquered and oppressed by a foreign enemy.

  - This literary pattern leads to the impression that gaining a toehold in the Promised Land took several generations. It was the result of a gradual settlement of the land, achieved in part through conquests and in part through treaties with local inhabitants.

  - The identity of "Israel" as a collective people made up of twelve tribes was likewise gradually achieved. Over generations of intermittent military and economic cooperation, a sense of national identity and shared origins emerged.

    o   One consistent feature in both accounts is the Israelite god. Whatever unity is achieved among these tribes is achieved through a shared allegiance to this national deity.

Biblical versus Near Eastern Archaeology

- In the 1920s and 1930s, scholars sought to prove the veracity of the Bible by lining up biblical stories with evidence from the archaeological record. Joshua's story of dramatic conquests of walled cities formed an ideal testing ground for this biblical archaeology.

In the early 1930s, the discovery of a collapsed wall at the site of Jericho seemed to highlight the accuracy of Joshua's account of conquest in Canaan.

    o   Biblical archaeologists began to locate and excavate the cities listed as "utterly destroyed" in the book of Joshua. They wanted to find evidence for a destruction layer in each of these cities that dated to around the 13th century B.C.E. The early results of this effort, such as the discovery of a collapsed wall at Jericho, seemed encouraging.

    o   As archaeological methods improved, however—specifically, the dating of stratigraphic layers in an archaeological site—little supporting evidence was found for Joshua's account of a massive military campaign in the land of Canaan.

- More recent archaeological approaches have shifted the focus from Israel in particular and the Bible's version of history to the region as a whole and what large-scale shifts in populations can tell us about the transition from the Late Bronze Age to the early Iron Age.

o We have already mentioned the Late Bronze Age collapse of the Canaanite city-states that controlled the central plains. We also noted the arrival of a new group of people along the coast, the Philistines, who were part of a larger migration of Sea Peoples from the area around Cypress to the coasts of Canaan and Egypt.

o Archaeology attests to both of these historical shifts of people and settlements.

- A new type of evidence comes from surface surveys of the land area on both sides of the Jordan River. Rather than excavate particular sites associated with the book of Joshua, archaeologists have documented where and when new settlements were founded in the region that eventually became ancient Israel. They discovered several significant patterns that help provide evidence for the origins of ancient Israel

o Beginning around 1200 B.C.E., a significant number of new settlements began to appear in the central highlands of the land of Canaan. The scale of this population increase cannot be explained through natural population growth but only by an influx of outsiders.

o These new settlements were concentrated in the central highlands, what the Bible labels as the territories of Manasseh and Ephraim, and in the Gilead and Moab across the Jordan. Almost all the settlements were founded on sites where there had been no previous occupation.

o The type of settlement is also different. Whereas the Late Bronze Age featured large, walled city-states, the new highland settlements were small, unwalled villages. This, of course, agrees with the evidence of the Merneptah Stele, which identifies "Israel" as a people rather than a walled city or territory.

- o Amidst all this newness—new population sources, new geographic regions, and new types of settlements—the material culture, meaning the types of pottery and other artifacts found in the new sites, suggests continuity with the Canaanite cities of the plains.

- o A second piece of evidence that suggests cultural and ethnic connections between the new settlers in the highlands and the Canaanites is language. Hebrew is a West Semitic language that is closely related to the Canaanite language, and it's nearly indistinguishable from the languages of Edom, Moab, and Ammon.

- The population increase suggests that outside groups must have settled the highlands of Canaan, and Israel's own stories of origin suggest that the Israelites came from Mesopotamia. But the material culture of these settlements and the fact that Hebrew is a West Semitic language suggest that the new settlers in the highlands were related to the Canaanites who had lived in the city-states.

- Where has archaeology brought us in our quest to find the origins of ancient Israel?
  - o It has disproved Joshua's version of a one-time, spectacularly successful military campaign to conquer the land of Canaan. It further suggests that the account in Judges of a gradual settlement punctuated by periodic military skirmishes is closer to historical reality.

  - o In this second version, a sense of Israelite national identity was achieved over time. Economic and military cooperation, intermarriage, and a shared allegiance to a national god all contributed to the forging of a new nation that came to understand itself as descendants of the twelve sons of Jacob.

Suggested Reading

Dever, *The Lives of Ordinary People in Ancient Israel*, pp. 106–205.

Kessler, *The Social History of Ancient Israel*, pp. 40–62.

Stager, "Forging an Identity," in Coogan, ed., *The Oxford History of the Biblical World*, pp. 90–131.

Questions to Consider

1. What might Joshua's story of a spectacular military victory over the land of Canaan have meant to the community of Judean exiles that preserved it?

2. From a modern perspective, how do we handle the view put forward in Joshua that military battles are led by God?

3. As a nation of immigrants, the United States is also a nation where national identity was achieved over time. Can you think of any immigrant stories where gradually, over generations, a family came to see itself as American? What events contribute to the development of a national identity?

Kinship and Economics in Rural Highland Villages
Lecture 6

In the last lecture, we noted that archaeological surveys of the central highlands of ancient Israel showed a marked increase in new settlements during the period 1200 to 1000 B.C.E. Traveling to one of these ancient villages would involve hiking up a series of steep, rocky hills. Once at the village, a visitor would see closely built clusters of mud-brick homes opening onto a shared courtyard. In this lecture, we'll explore an Israelite house in one of these highland settlements and see how the Israelites would have raised crops, prepared food, and shared resources to survive in this land. We'll also look to the biblical text to get a sense of the ancient Israelite family and village structure.

An Ancient Israelite House

- The rectangular pillared house was the dominant house type for all of Israelite history from 1200 B.C.E. to the exile in the 6th century B.C.E. The entrance was located at one of the narrow ends of the rectangle, opening to a large, pillared common area, or "broad room." This room and, possibly, an adjacent one would be used as the main activity area of the home.

- Such homes were constructed of sunbaked mud brick that was then plastered over. The thickness of the foundation walls and the discovery of the remains of staircases in some houses have led archaeologists to believe that many of these homes had two stories. The second story likely functioned as the main living area, where sleeping, dining, and some work, such as weaving, would have occurred. Recall that in the story of the widow of Zarephath, the sleeping space in her home was on the second story.

- The artifact assemblage in an individual pillared house suggests a high level of cooperation and subsistence living, a lifestyle in which men and women each made significant contributions to the survival of the family.

- o The pottery commonly found in pillared houses is simple, utilitarian, and unadorned. It consists mostly of cooking pots, serving vessels, and storage jars.

- o The enormous amount of space devoted to large storage jars suggests that there were entire seasons when the family would have to live off what they had harvested and stored.

- o The presence of stables inside the house points to the importance of animals and animal products, such as milk, wool, goat hair, and cowhides, for the livelihood of the rural family.

- o The common presence of loom weights for weaving indicates that families produced their own clothing and floor mats.

- Pillared houses are not found in isolation but connected to other houses, somewhat similar to a modern row of townhomes. A senior couple might occupy one pillared house, and adult sons and their families would occupy additional dwellings. All the houses would open onto a shared courtyard. There is strong evidence that these extended family compounds shared resources, such as ovens for baking, olive presses, and cisterns.

The Bible as a Window into Family Life
- Several biblical stories help us piece together what family life was like for the inhabitants of highland villages. First, we can say that family itself, especially a large family, was considered a tremendous blessing.

- Psalm 128 describes the life of a blessed man, a man who has revered the Lord and walked in his ways. In addition to being able to produce his own food in adequate quantities, the blessed man is one whose wife produces many children. The psalm closes with a wish for continued blessing for this man: "May you see your children's children."

o This psalm describes an idealized vision of rural family life set in one of the highland villages.

o A rural farming family is self-sufficient, living off what its members can produce with their own hands.

o The wife is likened to a vine and the children to olive shoots, both of which reflect two of the main crops produced in the highlands: grapes and olives.

o A crowd of children around one's table would be a blessing for a farming family that depends on the work of many hands.

o Finally, living to see a third generation on the land would ensure the continuation of a man's house, name, and monument.

- The gendered labor division reflected in Psalm 128 is also found in the story of the first couple in the Garden of Eden. The first man is created from the earth for the purposes of tending it.
  o The word for the man in Hebrew is *'ha'adam*. When we read in Genesis 2:7, "The Lord God formed the man of dust from the earth," the Hebrew employs a pun to show the connection between the man and the earth. The Hebrew reads in part, "The Lord God formed the *adam* from dust of the *adamah*." From the moment of his forming, the man is associated with the earth.

  o The woman is created last of all creatures. She is created out of the man's rib as a "helper" to him, but the text remains unclear about exactly what role is envisioned here. Still, the text suggests that her purpose, like that of the wife in Psalm 128, might be reproductive: "Therefore a man leaves his father and his mother and cleaves to his wife, and the two become one flesh."

  o As is well known from this story, there was one tree, the Tree of the Knowledge of Good and Evil, that was forbidden to the couple. When the couple ate the fruit of this tree and their transgression was discovered, God issued a series of punishments in which we see the same gendered association of the man with farming and the woman with childbearing.

- In both the psalm that describes the blessed man and the story of the creation of the first human couple, the Bible imagines a division of labor in which the man tills the soil and the woman produces children.
  - There is no doubt that life in the central highland villages involved working with one's hands and struggling to get the dry hillsides to produce crops.

  - It is also clear that women would spend most of their adult lives pregnant or nursing children. In order to have two children survive to adulthood, a woman might need as many as six pregnancies that resulted in live births.

  - Still, a simple division of labor where men work the fields and women produce babies at home does not find support in other parts of the Bible or in the archaeological record.

The Bible's Definition of "Family"

- There are two important Hebrew terms for "family": *bayit*, usually translated as "house," and *bet 'ab*, translated as "house of the father."
  - In English, the word "house" signifies the physical dwelling we live in. We have a separate word, "family," that

In the Genesis story, God's punishments of Adam and Eve exhibit gendered associations: men with tilling the soil and women with bearing children.

© Getty Images/Photos.com/Thinkstock.

describes the people to whom we are related. In biblical Hebrew, *bayit* signifies both a physical dwelling place and the group of people who reside in that dwelling place.

o The common extension of *bayit* is *bet 'ab*, "house of the father." This is the biblical designation for an extended family made up of a father, his wife or wives, his adult sons and their wives and children, unmarried sisters and daughters, slaves, and dependent workers.

• In Judges 17–18, we find an interesting description of a house and family, the *bayit* of a man named Micah. At one point, the household of Micah consists of himself, his mother, his son, and a salaried Levite priest. The description of Micah's house indicates that it was actually made up of several buildings, also called houses. In other words, it was probably akin to the shared family compounds that have been found archaeologically in the highland villages.

Division of Labor in the Bible

• The archaeological record, together with written and iconographic sources, supports a gendered division of labor, but it in no way limits a woman's economic value to reproduction.

• Farming and the herding of animals were men's work. At certain times of the year, the entire family, including children, would be involved in the work of planting and harvesting, but the Bible associates the production of the raw materials for bread, weaving, and wine making with men and the processing of those materials with women. The book of Isaiah (28:24–27) provides a fairly detailed picture of the process of farming from planting to threshing.

• Women's work included baking, weaving, and beer making, all of which were likely communal activities, with several women from an extended family compound working together. Bread making, in particular, was centrally important to the survival of the family.

o Carol Meyers, an archaeologist who has focused much of her research on the lives of ancient Israelite women, suggests that the average woman would have devoted a minimum of two hours each day to bread production, and others have suggested as many as five hours a day.

- o Millstones are commonly found in the broad rooms of ancient houses. They consist of a large, concave base stone and a smaller, convex upper stone that would be pushed forward over the grain to remove the husk and grind the seed into bread flour. The presence of several sets of grinding stones in the broad room of a single pillared house suggests that grinding grain was a communal activity.

- o The Bible gives us several examples of bread making by women. For example, when divine visitors come to Abraham to announce that his wife Sarah will give birth to a son in his old age, Abraham hastens to prepare a feast for the visitors. He rushes to the tent and tells his wife, "Make ready quickly three measures of fine meal, knead it and make cakes" (Gen. 18:6).

- Another activity that is consistently associated with women is weaving. Like bread making, this was an extremely time-consuming task.
  - o Cloth production within a household for common use is an excellent example of both subsistence living and the cooperative nature of men's and women's work in the highland villages.

  - o The wool or goat hair used to make threads came from the family's livestock. Men would shear the sheep in the spring, and women and girls would wash the wool and spin it into thread using a spindle and whorl. Then, the more senior, skilled women would weave the threads into clothing, sleeping mats, tents, and more. All these items would immediately be put to use in the household that produced them.

  - o Weaving was done on a vertical loom made of wood. Although such looms don't survive, small loom weights, used to keep the threads on the loom taut, are often found in courtyards, where women probably gathered during the dry season to weave and grind grains.

Suggested Reading

Ebeling, *Women's Lives in Biblical Times.*

King and Stager, *Life in Biblical Israel*, pp. 1–84.

Meyers, *Rediscovering Eve*, pp. 59–146.

Questions to Consider

1. How does an image of the physical structure of the Israelite house help you imagine what life was like in the highland villages? What details surprise you?

2. What does the structure of a shared family compound tell us about the relationships of the people who lived in that compound?

3. Does the story of Adam and Eve in the Garden of Eden suggest a divinely ordained division of labor between men and women?

Three Weddings and a Funeral
Lecture 7

In the last lecture, we looked at the ancient Israelite home and learned how the members of extended families cooperated with one another to farm in a difficult landscape. In this lecture, we'll look at some of the practices and beliefs that surrounded marriage in ancient Israel. Our primary source for this exploration will be the book of Genesis. Even though the stories in Genesis are set during the time before Israel became a nation, they were written much later, during the time when Israel existed as a monarchy. Thus, the marriage practices we find in the stories of Genesis likely reflect the ideals of Israel as a nation and a kingdom during the Iron Age.

The Marriage of Isaac and Rebekah
- The marriage of Isaac and Rebekah in Genesis 24 is a good starting point for our study because it provides our most complete description of a betrothal, and it conforms to the type of marriage that ancient Israel considered ideal.
  - The ideal marriage was patrilocal, meaning that a woman married out of her own family's home into her husband's household.

  - It was also endogamous, meaning that the husband and wife were from the same extended family or clan.

  - Finally, an ideal marriage was negotiated between the families of the bride and groom for their mutual long-term benefit.

- The first thing we notice when we read the betrothal story of Isaac and Rebekah is that Isaac isn't present. Abraham, Isaac's father, has grown old and wants to see his son settled. He sends his servant back to his homeland in Mesopotamia to acquire a wife for Isaac.

- The servant travels to Haran, and once there, he waits by the village well in the evening, when the women will come to draw water. The ideal wife for Isaac appears immediately. The text identifies the woman as Abraham's grandniece; thus, the marriage would fit the criterion of endogamy. We also learn that Rebekah is beautiful and a virgin, and she is a willing worker. The servant gives Rebekah a gold ring and two bracelets, the first in a series of bridal gifts that he will transfer to Rebekah and her family.

- At this point, the story's location shifts to Rebekah's mother's house. The term "mother's house" is used only four times in the Bible and only in the context of marriage. This suggests that a bride's mother and, as we'll see, her brother played key roles in negotiating a marriage for a daughter.
  - Rebekah's brother Laban emerges as the consummate host. He invites the servant into the house, sees to the care of the camels, and prepares a feast. Before the servant will eat, he tells Laban and the others that he has come to find a wife for Abraham's son Isaac. One of the key details he shares with this group of relatives is that Abraham has become wealthy in the land of Canaan.

  - Laban and his father, Bethuel, immediately agree to the proposal. The appearance of Rebekah's father in a place called her "mother's house" has caused consternation for biblical commentators. Some believe it is a mistake, but it could be that within the extended family compound of Bethuel, a dwelling might be designated for Rebekah, Laban, and their mother. What's significant is that the betrothal feast is consumed and the marriage itself proposed and accepted in the mother's house.

  - After the proposal is accepted, the servant bestows wedding gifts on Rebekah, Laban, and her mother. These gifts are meant to compensate the family for the loss of their daughter, but they also serve as a testimony to the wealth of Abraham and Isaac.

Before leaving her mother's house to travel to Canaan, Rebekah receives a blessing from her mother and brother: that she may have fertility, strength, and power over enemies in her new land.

- o Interestingly, when the servant insists that he would like to leave on the return journey immediately, Rebekah is asked whether she is willing to go. In other words, the bride is given a choice. Rebekah responds, "I will go."

- We then fast forward to Rebekah's arrival at Isaac's village and his first appearance in the story. The text tells us: "Isaac brought her into his mother's tent, and took Rebekah, and she became his wife; and he loved her." Once again, the marriage and consummation take place in a space associated with the mother, suggesting that mothers played important roles in arranging marriages.

- One aspect of this marriage that becomes clear in later chapters is that it joins two families across generations. In this preferred marriage type in ancient Israel, the families who negotiate the marriage form new kinship bonds that will extend through multiple generations.

The Marriage of Hagar and Abram

- The marriage of Hagar and Abram is described in Genesis 16. The backdrop for this story is the barrenness of Abraham's wife Sarah. Because of this, Sarai (Sarah) offers her slave-girl Hagar to Abram (Abraham). Immediately, we note several details that distinguish this type of marriage from the type we saw negotiated for Isaac and Rebekah.
  - First, it will be a plural marriage.

  - It is entered into for the express purpose of obtaining children because the first wife was unable to bear children.

  - It is not endogamous because Hagar is Egyptian.

  - Perhaps most significantly, it is negotiated not by Hagar's family for her benefit but by Hagar's mistress, Sarah, for Sarah's benefit.

  - The phrase Sarah uses to describe her motivation for the marriage is "perhaps I will obtain children through her." The Hebrew verb *'ibbaneh*, which is translated as "obtain children," also means "to be built up." Sarah imagines that she can be built up in the house of her husband if her slave-girl can produce an heir for her.

- Abram listens to Sarai and takes Hagar as a "wife." The word for "wife" here is the same one used to describe Sarah as Abram's wife and Rebekah as Isaac's wife. It is only through the circumstances of the marriage that we learn that Hagar is a different kind of wife who will have a different status from Sarai in Abram's household.

- o Unlike Sarai, Hagar immediately conceives, and then, "she looked with contempt on her mistress."

- o Sarai feels betrayed by her slave-girl and by Abram. But when she complains, Abram lets her know that she is the one in control of this aspect of the household. He says, "Look, your slave-girl is in your power, do to her as you please" (Gen. 16:6).

- o We then read that Sarai dealt harshly with Hagar, and Hagar fled the house into the wilderness.

- Again, we note several differences in the marriage of Hagar and Abraham from that of Isaac and Rebekah. Hagar's family is not involved in the marriage negotiations, and therefore, Hagar's interests are not protected. Sarai negotiates Hagar's change in status from slave-girl to wife, and she does this so that she, not Hagar, can be "built up" in Abram's household. Even after Hagar conceives, she remains a foreign slave under the power of Sarai.

- Later, in Genesis 21, Sarai miraculously conceives and bears her own son, Isaac. As soon as she weans Isaac, she expels Hagar and her son, Ishmael, from Abraham's household. Hagar has no rights to Abraham's estate. Deuteronomy 21:15 provides a law that seems designed to deal with disputes involving two wives and two firstborn sons, but it may address a situation in which the wives are of equal status.

Dinah: Marriage by Abduction
- In Genesis 34, we read, "Dinah, the daughter of Leah, whom she bore to Jacob, went out to visit the women of the land." While she was out, Shechem, the prince of the land, "saw her, seized her, and lay with her by force." He then apparently takes her back to his house before initiating negotiations with her family to make her his wife.

- Note that this marriage is not endogamous; Shechem is of another nation. Note, too, that the marriage is not negotiated in a way that allows the daughter's interests to be protected. Instead, after

Shechem has sexually claimed Dinah, he negotiates for marriage. As appalling as this story strikes us now, the law concerning rape at this time was that the rapist was obligated to marry the woman he violated and pay her father 50 shekels (Deut. 22:28–29).

- Another form of marriage by abduction occurs as an act of war. In Deuteronomy 21:10–14, Israelite men who go to war are told that they may take the enemy's women as their captives. The law stipulates that if the man is later displeased with this wife, he cannot sell her for money or treat her as a slave, but he may release her.

Lives of Women in Ancient Israel

- These three types of weddings attested in the Bible point to several conclusions about the lives of women in ancient Israel.

- For a wife to have some degree of power in her husband's household, she must have entered that household through a proper set of family negotiations. A woman's brothers were especially important in securing her place of prestige in her husband's household.

- To be fully secure in her husband's household, a wife also had to produce an heir. If she could not, she could arrange for a secondary wife through which her husband could obtain an heir.

- Foreign slave women and captive women were more vulnerable because they had no families to secure their rights.

- A wife's status in the household of her husband affected the status of her sons. The law designed to protect the son of the "hated wife" speaks to a reality in which the sons of hated wives were often disinherited.

The Funeral of Abraham

- In Genesis 25:7, we learn that Abraham died at the age of 175 years. Isaac and Ishmael, Abraham's two sons from Sarah and Hagar, bury him in a cave with his primary wife, Sarah. The listing of Isaac before Ishmael here is significant.

- Before Abraham dies, he settles his estate with his sons.
  - After Sarah's death, Abraham had arranged a third marriage for himself with Keturah, who bore him six additional sons.

  - But it is Isaac, the son of the ideal type of wife, who will be the sole inheritor of Abraham's estate. We read: "Abraham gave all he had to Isaac. But to the sons of his concubines Abraham gave gifts" (Gen. 25:5–6). The label "concubine" clarifies that Hagar and Keturah and their offspring have a lesser status than Sarah and Isaac.

- This story of Abraham's death and burial makes it clear that Abraham's land and wealth are tied through marriage to Sarah and her offspring. Only Sarah will merit burial in the family cave with Abraham, and only Isaac will inherit the land of his father.

Suggested Reading

Meyers, *Rediscovering Eve*, pp. 59–146.

Steinberg, *Kinship and Marriage in Genesis*, pp. 5–86.

Questions to Consider

1. When you read Genesis 16, what phrases or labels illustrate the status differentiation among Abram, Sarai, and Hagar?

2. Based on the stories of marriages in Genesis, what factors contributed to a woman's power and prestige in the house of her husband? What factors lowered her status?

3. How might a son's ability to inherit affect the life of his mother in her old age?

Political Power Bases in Early Israel
Lecture 8

In this lecture, we will look at political power bases in ancient Israel dating to the time of the Judges, 1200–1000 B.C.E. During this period, various men and at least one woman rose to power in time of military crisis. Their primary function was to deliver the Israelites from foreign rule, which they did with the support of their national deity. These leaders also adjudicated disputes between people and clans. In addition to the judges, two other significant centers of power were known at this time: the elders, representing a kinship-based system of leadership that exercised authority at the clan and tribal level, and the king, a type of ruler known among the small nations that battled Israel.

The Book of Judges
- Judges contains a collection of stories about miraculous and colorful leaders. These figures include:
  o Ehud, a left-handed Benjaminite (the name Benjamin means "son of my right hand") whose left-handed swordsmanship delivers a lethal blow to an enemy Moabite king.

  o Deborah, the single female judge, who together with Barak, defeats the army of Sisera but leaves the final victory to another woman, Yael, who hammers a tent peg through Sisera's head.

  o Jephthah, who utters a rash oath to God in an effort to guarantee a military victory and ends up having to sacrifice his only child, a daughter.

  o Samson, the strong man who is brought low by Delilah; in shearing him of his long hair, she also shears him of his strength.

- These legendary stories probably circulated independently before being collected in their current form in the book of Judges.

- Territorially, the stories are distinct, and the enemies in these stories vary, but they are all local enemies, similar in size and military power to Israel. Also like Israel, its enemies—the Moabites, Ammonites, Philistines, and Canaanites—had their own national deities who were thought to protect them and lead them in battle.

Deuteronomistic History in Judges

- The book of Judges is associated with an editorial pattern called the "Deuteronomistic history." Writers in this vein are thought to have edited the history of ancient Israel in the books of Joshua, Judges, 1 and 2 Samuel, and 1 and 2 Kings. What ties the editorial framework of these books together is a worldview and system of values that echo the book of Deuteronomy.

- The editorial pattern of this history in the book of Judges begins with a declaration that "the people of Israel did what was evil in the sight of the Lord and served the Ba'als; and they forsook the Lord, the God of their fathers" (Judg. 2:11–12).

- Because the people have turned to foreign gods, "the anger of the Lord was kindled against Israel, and he gave them over to plunderers … he sold them into the power of their enemies" (Judg. 2:14). The enemies defeat and oppress Israel for a period until Israel finally "cries out to the Lord" for deliverance.

- Then we read: "The Lord raised up judges who saved them out of the power of those who plundered them" (Judg. 2:16). In other words, the Israelite god hears the cries of his people and responds by raising up a judge who can deliver them out of the hands of their enemies. Once the Israelite god has chosen a man to become a judge, this fact is communicated through a formula: "The spirit of the Lord" rushes upon the man, and he becomes capable of great military feats.

- Returning to the generalized description of a judge in chapter 2, we are told something about the tenure of a judge's leadership: "Whenever the Lord raised up judges for them, the Lord was with the judge and he saved them from the hand of their enemies all the days of the judge." In other words, judges are guaranteed rulership for their lifetimes only; once they die, the editorial pattern of the Deuteronomistic history repeats itself.

Deborah
- The introduction of Deborah's rule in Judges 4 follows the pattern of the Deuteronomistic history. The people of Israel had done evil in the sight of the Lord, had been oppressed, and had cried out for help.

- But Deborah is the only judge who does not come to power by achieving a military victory over Israel's enemies. Instead, she is already acting as judge when a military crisis arises, and she responds to the need to defeat the Canaanites.

- In this introduction to Deborah's story, we also find a description of another aspect of being a judge: Deborah offers judgments to people who come before her "court"—a palm tree.

Jephthah
- Many of the judges are introduced in ways that suggest they have some sort of disadvantage that they then use to gain the upper hand. For Jephthah, this disadvantage is his birth: He is the son of a prostitute and a man named Gilead, who also had legitimate sons. Jephthah is forced to flee his half-brothers and dwell in the land of Tob. There, a group of "worthless fellows" gathers around him, and he takes them out on raids. Although this is hardly a model occupation, Jephthah is described as a "mighty warrior."

- When the Ammonites come to fight against Israel, the legitimate sons of Gilead are not up to the challenge; a different authoritative group steps in: "the elders of Gilead." These elders search out Jephthah to bring him back to fight against the Ammonites. Jephthah agrees if the elders will make him their leader.

- In Judges 11:29, we read, "the spirit of the Lord came upon Jephthah." This formulaic language signifies that he has been raised up by the Israelite god, and with his god's help, he will be able to achieve the military victory he needs over the Ammonites.

- o Jephthah seeks further assurance of victory by making a vow to his god; he promises that if he returns victorious, whoever first comes from his house to meet him will be given to the Lord as a burnt offering.

- o Of course, Jephthah defeats the Ammonites and returns home victorious, only to be met by his daughter. She agrees to submit to the terms of the vow but asks for a reprieve of two months so that she and her female companions can go to the mountains to bewail her virginity. When she returns, Jephthah "did with her according to his vow" (Judg. 11:39).

Judges gives us a brief note supporting the existence of a women's pilgrimage ritual in memory of the daughter of Jephthah.

- The closing note on Jephthah's career as judge is that he judged Israel for six years and then died and was buried in Gilead.

- From Jephthah's tenure as a judge, we learn that the primary function of this office was to deliver Israel militarily from its enemies. It is this military deliverance that, in almost all cases, inaugurates a person's status as judge. Because the office of the judge is brought on by the onrush of the spirit of the Lord and comes to a close at the person's death, this type of leadership is often called "charismatic leadership."

Elders and Kings in the Book of Judges

- Elders were heads of families that acted as leaders at the level of an extended clan or tribe. In the case of Jephthah's story, they are leaders over the tribe of Gilead. Their power was firmly embedded in the kinship structure and limited to their own geographic area.
  - Elders did not hold a particular office but, rather, were convened as needed to deal with issues of importance.

  - In the period of the Judges, the elders seem to execute judgments and act as problem solvers on the local level; they also act as intermediaries between the people and the judges who rule them.

- Kings are often referred to in the book of Judges, but they are almost always kings of the surrounding nations against which Israel goes to war. When we read about "kings of Israel" in the book of Judges, we realize that we are reading a retrospective history. In other words, the story of the Judges is told from a historical vantage point that has known kingship and the monarchy in Israel.
  - The first way the concept of kingship enters the book of Judges is through the repeated assertion "In those days there was no king in Israel and everyone did what was right in his own eyes." This pronouncement implies that the period of the Judges was a time of anarchy, only brought back to order through kingship. Because such references are clustered at the end of the book, they create a kind of drumbeat that suggests the rule of the judges is failing and the time for kingship is at hand.

  - The second way in which the concept of kingship in Israel is introduced in the book of Judges is through the career of the judge Gideon, whose story brings together a discussion of the judge, the elders, and the king.

Anticipating Kingship: Gideon

- Gideon's rise to power as a judge contains all the elements of the traditional pattern in Judges. For the evil they have done, the Lord hands the Israelites over to the power of Midian, where they are oppressed for seven years. The Israelites cry out for help, and ultimately, the spirit of the Lord "take[s] possession of Gideon" (Judg. 6:34), and he defeats the Midianites. Gideon then rules as judge for 40 years.

- We've come to expect these stock elements in the framing of a judge's career, but there are several features that suggest Gideon's judgeship was different.
    o The key difference comes in chapter 8, after Gideon has subdued the Midianite threat. A group referred to as "the men of Israel"—perhaps the elders—comes to Gideon and suggests the establishment of a dynastic rule instead of the customary charismatic rule that would end when the judge dies.

    o Gideon's response indicates that he fully understands that this request is for a different kind of leadership. He says, "I will not rule over you, and my son will not rule over you; the Lord will rule over you." Thus, from the perspective of this story, dynastic rule within a human family is an affront to the Israelite god, whom Gideon sees as the only legitimate ruler in perpetuity over Israel.

- Still, several details in the story of Gideon suggest that his righteous rejection of dynastic rule may be only one side of his story. He builds a shrine in his hometown, levies taxes, takes multiple wives, and gives one of his sons a royal name, all of which suggests that there may have been something monarchic in Gideon's rule.

Suggested Reading

Ackerman, *Warrior, Dancer, Seductress, Queen.*

Brettler, *The Book of Judges.*

1. Although aspects of the book of Judges are clearly fantastical, how might this book reflect genuine aspects of political developments that occurred just prior to the beginning of the Israelite monarchy?

2. In what ways might the stories of individual judges function as entertainment? Where can you imagine these stories being told orally?

Kingdoms and King Making
Lecture 9

With this lecture, we begin a new unit on kings and kingdoms in Israel and Judah. Historically, this unit takes us into the first half of the period known as Iron Age II (1000–745 B.C.E.). We'll begin the unit with the rise of David as king over Israel (the united monarchy), and we'll close in 745, when the Assyrian Empire reappeared in the Levant and threatened the kingdoms of Israel and Judah (first half of the divided monarchy). In this unit, we will continue our investigation of political developments in ancient Israel; examine state-sponsored sanctuaries; and look at changes in class divisions brought about by the flourishing monarchies of northern Israel and southern Judah.

Overview of the Monarchy
- The Bible records the history of King David and the histories of the northern and southern kingdoms in 1 and 2 Samuel and 1 and 2 Kings. These books are part of the Deuteronomistic history, which was written centuries after David from the perspective of the southern kingdom of Judah.

- Saul was the first Israelite to be crowned king over all Israel, but he failed to establish a dynasty when he and his heir died in battle.

- David was not only crowned king over all Israel, but he passed the kingship to his son Solomon. Together, the reigns of these two men constitute the united monarchy.

- After the death of Solomon, the kingdom split, with the single tribe of Judah becoming the kingdom of Judah under Solomon's son Rehoboam and the northern tribes becoming the kingdom of Israel under Jeroboam.

Rise of the Monarchy

- One reason the nation of Israel shifted from a kinship-based society to a monarchic state may have been a rapid increase in population in the highland villages, which may have made a subsistence economy increasingly difficult to maintain. Pooling resources across villages and trading with cities in the plains would have helped address the food needs of this increased population. At the same time, this would require greater organizational structures.

- A second reason that ancient Israel developed into a monarchic state may have come from the persistent threat of the Philistines. These Sea Peoples had arrived on the southern coasts of Canaan at about the same time that Israel began to emerge as a people living in the villages of the central highlands.
  - o In the book of Judges, the Israelites always seemed to have a fighting chance against their enemies.

  - o At some point prior to monarchic rule in Israel, however, the Philistines emerged as a more significant and enduring threat, one that required a more organized approach than what a judge could provide.

Tribal Relationships and Kingship

- The tribal relationships we saw in Genesis and the book of Judges continue to serve as a backdrop to the Bible's presentation of kingship. Recall that Jacob was the eponymous ancestor of ancient Israel. He had twelve sons from four wives. These twelve sons became the twelve tribes of Israel.

- If we were to use Genesis as our predictor text, we would expect kingship to emerge from Ephraim, who was the chosen son of Joseph and the first son of Rachel, the wife whom Jacob loved. The book of Genesis closes with Joseph's death and the election of Ephraim, and later traditions suggest that kingship will first emerge in the northern territory of Ephraim.

- When we look at the history of kingship, we see a struggle between the descendants of Rachel and those of Leah. Significantly, none of the sons of the maidservant wives became contenders in either the priestly or the royal realms.

- In tracing the advent of kingship in Israel, note that tribal identities and divisions continue to exercise authority.
  - The tribal leadership structure of the elders plays a key role in anointing and unseating kings.

  - And the kingdom is conceptualized as a single house; the rulers are all descendants of the house of Jacob. At the same time, however, the house of Rachel and the house of Leah within the larger house of Jacob communicate the division between north and south.

- With the advent of the monarchy, we will also see new bases of power emerge that operate independently from the older tribal systems.

David and Solomon
- Social scientists associate certain features with an early state in contrast to a kinship-based society. These features include a centralized capital city, a standing army, a system of taxation, the use of conscripted labor, monumental buildings and public works projects, and the increased use of writing, which is then linked to the development of a royal theology. Let's explore the dynasty of David in light of these marks of monarchic rule.

- At the time of Saul's death, David was a military commander in his army. He traveled to Hebron, a city in his tribal territory of Judah. There, he was anointed king of Judah, his tribe. In other words, after the death of Saul, the people reverted to their tribal territories and allegiances.

- After seven years of ruling a single tribe, the "elders of Israel" come to David and anoint him king over all Israel. Once anointed, David sets out to secure the allegiance of "all Israel," and here, we begin to see new structures of authority emerge alongside the older tribal structures.

o David establishes a new capital in Jerusalem, a city not associated with any tribe. He then builds a royal palace there.

o David also brings the Ark of the Covenant to Jerusalem and installs it in a tent shrine. By moving the ark to Jerusalem, David is able to absorb the power of this sacred tribal cult object.

- Additional marks of monarchic rule are achieved when David's son Solomon comes to power. Solomon embarks on an ambitious building program that involves taxation and conscripted labor.

- One additional way to chart the development of an organized monarchic state is through the number and type of officials and functionaries that are mentioned in relationship to a king's reign.

o Saul had only one named official, the commander of his army. David also had a commander, as well as a recorder, a secretary, two priests, and a director of forced labor. In Solomon's rule, the palace apparatus included an army commander, multiple secretaries, a recorder, priests, and others.

o This growing list of titled jobs associated with the royal court marks an increasingly powerful state apparatus that operated independently of the earlier kinship-based power structures centered on elders and villages.

Jeroboam and the Northern Kingdom

- The story of the division of Israel into two kingdoms—the northern kingdom of Israel and the southern kingdom of Judah—is found in 1 Kings 11–12, and the episode is usually dated to around 928 B.C.E.

- At the death of Solomon, his son Rehoboam is set to succeed him as king of a united Israel. Rehoboam's choice of Shechem as the city for his anointing is an early sign that his power base is weak among the northern tribes.

- At the anointing ceremony, an Ephraimite named Jeroboam appears to challenge Rehoboam.
  - Jeroboam had served as the head of forced labor in Ephraim under Solomon, but when his power grew too great, Solomon sought to kill him, and Jeroboam had fled to Egypt.

  - Jeroboam returned to Israel when he heard that Solomon was dead. He now leads a group called the "assembly of Israel" to Rehoboam and requests that the new king "lighten the hard service" of his father (1 Kings 12:4). His request signals the discontent of the northern tribes with the forced labor arrangements established under Solomon.

- Rehoboam seeks council with two groups for advice on how to respond to Jeroboam: the elders who had served his father and the friends of his youth. Rather than take the elders' advice to lighten the people's load, Rehoboam listens to his friends and vows to place an even heavier burden on the people.

- In this moment of crisis and uncertainty, the people respond by reverting to the security of their tribes and the older power structures of the village elders. The phrase "To your tents, O Israel" is a command to return to their tribal territories and villages and withdraw from this effort at unity.

- In the end, Rehoboam was forced to return to Jerusalem, where he began his rule over the tribe of Judah only. Jeroboam was anointed king over "all Israel," now meaning the ten tribes.

- If we think again about the makeup of the household of Jacob, we see that the kingdom has divided along the lines of the maternal sub-houses. Jeroboam of Ephraim traces his ancestry to the house of Rachel, while Rehoboam of Judah traces his ancestry to the house of Leah. Although the two maternal houses conceptualize the split of the kingdom, the fact that they are understood to be housed within a larger house of Jacob asserts their enduring or, at least, intended unity.

Archaeological Evidence for the United Monarchy

- There are no independent references to David or Solomon outside of the Bible that date to the late 11th or 10th centuries, when these two men would have ruled. There is no independent attestation of a new kingdom of Israel in the 10th century in writings from Egypt or Mesopotamia.

The inscription on the Mesha Stele is important because it refers to Omri, a known king from the Bible, as "king of Israel."

- Our first extra-biblical references to a monarchy in ancient Israel date to the 9th century B.C.E., 100 years after Solomon.
  - The first piece of evidence comes in the form of an Aramaic inscription discovered in the archaeological site of Tel Dan in the north of Israel. The inscription refers, first, to a "king of Israel" and, second, to the "house of David." Thus, the inscription agrees with the biblical presentation of a divided monarchy in the 9th century, and it indicates that one of these kingdoms traced its origins to a figure named David. But it does not speak to the time of the united monarchy.

  - The second inscription, found on the Mesha Stele, is much more complete. This stone dates to around 830 B.C.E., during the time of the divided kingdom. It narrates events that are described biblically in 2 Kings 3, but it doesn't help us confirm any details about the united monarchy under David and Solomon.

Lecture 9: Kingdoms and King Making

- Another approach to uncover evidence for the united monarchy is to focus on the extensive building activity that the Bible credits to Solomon. One promising piece of evidence for a Solomonic kingdom is provided by the excavation of gate structures in the cities of Hazor, Megiddo, and Gezer, where Solomon is said to have built walls. However, finding scholarly consensus on the dates of these structures has proven difficult.

Suggested Reading

Coogan, *The Old Testament*, pp. 233–307.

Kessler, *The Social History of Ancient Israel*, pp. 63–102.

Questions to Consider

1. How does the Bible provide evidence for the development of a centralized bureaucracy during the time of the monarchy?

2. Why do you think the kinship-based leadership centered in the elders continued to exercise power even after the founding of a monarchy?

3. How does the genealogy of the house of Jacob found in Genesis inform the political divisions that we see during the time of the monarchy?

Politics and Economy of a Centralized Cult
Lecture 10

T he ancient Near East understood kingship as a gift from the gods. Kings ruled as human representatives of the divine realm, begotten by the gods and nursed by goddesses. Their directives were sponsored and supported by their national deities. We find a similar close association between king and god in the biblical presentation of David. One of the ways ancient Near Eastern kings publically expressed their closeness to the divine realm was through building temples to their sponsoring deities. In this lecture, we will look at these state-sponsored sanctuaries and explore the central economic role the temple would have played in the development of a monarchic state.

Divine Kingship
- The ancient Near East as a whole understood kingship as a political institution closely tied to the divine realm.
  - The Sumerian King List, a cuneiform text dating to the early 2nd millennium B.C.E., declares that kingship itself was an institution "lowered from heaven."

  - In the Epic of Gilgamesh, the ancient Mesopotamian king Gilgamesh was said to be "two-thirds god and one-third human."

  - The kings of the Neo-Assyrian Empire, beginning in the 9th century B.C.E., did not claim full divinity but always asserted divine sponsorship and guidance.

  - The royal enthronement texts of the Egyptian pharaohs list a series of throne names that culminate in the claim that the pharaoh is the "only begotten son" of the sun god Re.

- We also find a close association between king and god in the biblical presentation of David, particularly in the Royal Psalms.

These psalms in praise of the king are set within the temple and may have been used as part of an enthronement festival.

- One way in which ancient Near Eastern kings publically expressed their closeness to the divine realm was through building temples to their sponsoring deities. In our last lecture, we noted that immediately after being anointed king of all Israel, David brought the Ark of the Covenant, the footstool of the Israelite god, to his capital city in Jerusalem. His son Solomon then built a temple to house the Israelite god and placed his footstool within it.

Economic Role of the Temple

- In the account of Solomon's building of the temple, we learn that he had to tax families to pay for luxury materials from outside the kingdom and for the craftsman-quality labor needed for certain aspects of the temple. Already, there were economic ramifications on all the territories under Solomon's control.

- Once the Jerusalem temple was built, the requirement that all pilgrimage feasts take place there would have meant that people had to travel long distances, bypassing their local shrines, to come to Jerusalem. Worshipers would bring their sacrifices to the temple, and a portion of each sacrifice would serve the priests, with the rest coming back to the family.

- Because of the increased distance that people had to travel, bringing an animal from home for the purpose of sacrifice would have been difficult for some. As a result, over time, people were allowed to sell an animal in their home district and take the silver with them to Jerusalem to buy a calf or sheep or wine for use in the temple sacrifice. In this way, we see the gradual development of a money economy centered on the temple.

- The temple had its own treasury that was distinguished from the royal treasury. When the two are mentioned together, the temple treasury is listed first, suggesting that it is of greater importance and value. Still, the king had access to the funds in both treasuries.

Reconstructing the Jerusalem Temple

- No direct archaeological remains of the Solomonic temple have yet been uncovered.
  - In fact, after more than a century of extensive excavations in Jerusalem, archaeologists have not been able to identify any structures that would have been a part of the city of David, dating to the early 10th century.

  - The fact that Jerusalem continues to be a built-up, populated city makes wide-scale excavation impossible. What would have been the Temple Mount in Solomon's time currently houses the Al-Aqsa Mosque and the Dome of the Rock. Some archaeologists believe that the remains of a Solomonic temple lay buried beneath this modern sacred site.

- Without any archaeological remains, we are left with descriptions of the temple found in the Bible and comparative examples of Levantine temples dating to the early 1st millennium.
  - In 1 Kings 5–9, we find descriptions of the construction of the temple, including its measurements, materials used, and decorations. Also, in line with the royal theology of divine kingship, we learn that the temple was understood as the house of the Israelite god and the chapel of the king.

  - Ezekiel was a priest and a prophet during the time of the Babylonian Exile, and chapters 40–48 of his book record this priest's vision of a rebuilt, restored temple in Jerusalem. Although this is an idealized vision, some of its details suggest an accurate memory of the first temple and a similar ideological understanding of the temple as a dwelling place of God.

- Another source for reconstruction comes from outside the Bible. Archaeologists have excavated other early-1st-millennium Levantine temples that match the architectural plan and iconographic program of the Solomonic temple described in the Bible. Discoveries of various cult objects in shrines outside of Jerusalem are also helpful in reimagining the temple of Solomon.

Physical Structure of the Jerusalem Temple

- The Jerusalem temple was a rectangular structure measuring 165 by 85 feet and divided into three rooms. It was a "straight axis" temple with an east-west orientation and was surrounded by an inner and an outer courtyard.

- As one approached the temple, concentric courtyards marked the movement into increasingly sacred space.
    - In the inner courtyard was a huge bronze basin or tank called *yam* ("sea"). The basin, which presumably held water, was mounted on the backs of twelve bronze oxen.

    - Also in the courtyard were ten large bronze cult stands that are described as having "panels set in frames," and "in the frames were lions, oxen and cherubim" (1 Kings 7:28–29). Each stand was placed on "four bronze wheels." Surrounding sites have produced religious objects that match this description, suggesting the reliability of the biblical account.

- The temple itself was considered the dwelling place of the Israelite god; thus, the average pilgrim to Jerusalem would never enter it. Because the temple was understood on the model of a house, it is not surprising that many of its architectural features reflect the ancient Israelite house complex.
    - We've already noted that both the temple and the pillared house were rectangular, with the entrance on the narrow end. The surrounding courtyard would be a second shared feature. The outer courtyard of the temple would be where people gathered.

    - The entrance to the temple was marked by two bronze pillars with ornately decorated capitals. Only priests would enter through these pillars into the first room, a vestibule, and then on into the main room.

    - The main room was decorated with cedar paneling; cypress floorboards; and carvings of palm trees, flowers, and cherubim.

The account in Kings repeatedly emphasizes that the surfaces of seemingly everything were overlaid with gold.

o The innermost room of the sanctuary is referred to as the Holy of Holies. In this room, Solomon is said to have placed the Ark of the Covenant, marking the place symbolically as the throne room of the deity. Our best description of the Holy of Holies comes from the prophet and priest Isaiah (Isa. 6), who describes receiving his commission to prophesy while standing in this room.

Ideological Role of the Temple

- The account of Solomon's dedication of the temple shows how a royal sanctuary served as a uniting point for the kingdom and legitimized Solomon's rule.
  - o The invitation list for this royal dedication ceremony (1 Kings 8:1) shows the king's desire to win over the tribal leadership of the elders.

  - o While the priests carry the ark and all its accompanying cultic objects to the new temple, Solomon is described as offering countless animal sacrifices before the ark. The priests then placed the ark within the Holy of Holies.

  - o In both Isaiah's account and the description of the dedication, we get a sense that ancient Israelites imagined their deity as enormous. The ark was nothing more than his footstool, and his head was somewhere in the heavens. The hem of his robe filled the entire temple. His presence in the form of "glory" filled the temple like a cloud.

- Another way in which the temple served as a legitimizing feature of a king's rule was in its proximity to the royal palace and its architectural mirroring of the king's throne room. In a sense, the temple and palace shared a courtyard, suggesting that the king was part of the extended family compound of the deity. Both palace and temple also shared the same architectural layout and iconographic representations.

Syrian Temples of the 1st Millennium

- According to Kings, Solomon engaged Hiram, king of Tyre, to assist in building the temple in Jerusalem. This connection to the northern territory of Syria around Tyre makes the excavation of two Syrian temples dating to the early 1st millennium especially helpful in reconstructing the Solomonic temple. The two excavated temples are at sites called Tell Ta'yinat and 'Ain Dara'.

- Both of these temples are rectangular buildings divided into three rooms, with the entrance on the narrow end and the Holy of Holies on the far end. Both were also built adjacent to larger palace complexes. The iconography in the 'Ain Dara' temple closely adheres to that described for Solomon's temple in the Bible.

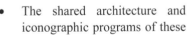

© Verity Cridland/Wikimedia Commons/CC BY 2.0.

- One additional find that is very suggestive is a series of enormous footprints incised into the floor panels at the entrance to the 'Ain Dara' temple. Placed in sequence, they suggest that the deity stood at the pillared entrance to his temple and then walked in.

The entrance to the temple at 'Ain Dara' was marked by stairs, winged cherubim, and a pair of sculpted lions whose bodies served as the bases for two pillars.

- The shared architecture and iconographic programs of these Syrian temples with what 1 Kings and Ezekiel describe as the Solomonic temple suggest that the biblical account is reliable in its detail, though not necessarily in its dating.

- Ancient Israelites would have understood the Jerusalem temple as the house of their god. They would know that the Ark of the Covenant was placed within it as the earthly footstool of their god. The role of the king in building the temple, installing the ark, and dedicating the temple would have forcefully communicated his status as the anointed one, a divine son, the earthly representative of the Israelite god.

Suggested Reading

Dever, *The Lives of Ordinary People in Ancient Israel*, pp. 249–293.

King and Stager, *Life in Biblical Israel*, pp. 319–362.

Stavrakopoulou and Barton, eds., *Religious Diversity in Ancient Israel and Judah*, pp. 61–81.

Questions to Consider

1. How does the architecture and iconography of the temple at 'Ain Dara' help us to understand and imagine the Solomonic temple?

2. Why did David, Solomon, and Jeroboam prioritize the building of state-sponsored temples?

3. How did the ancient Israelites imagine their god? What specific details in the temple's architecture and furnishings help you to answer this question?

Worshipping Locally
Lecture 11

In our last lecture, we talked about the intersection of religion, politics, and the economy that we find expressed in state-sponsored royal temples. Monumental temples embodied royal efforts to centralize and control worship and, ultimately, to control the flow of economic goods that accompanied the sacrificial cult. Although many Israelites likely stood in awe of these massive temples in the north and south, there is no indication that the centralized royal cult ever succeeded in eliminating local religious practices. In this lecture, we will look at the tremendous diversity in ancient Israelite religious practice documented in the Bible.

Biblical Perspective on Religious Diversity

- The Bible's constant proclamations forbidding the worship of any god except for the Israelite god and the calls to worship only in Jerusalem suggest the continuation of local religious practices.
  - We find the command for the exclusive worship of the Israelite god at the very beginning of the Ten Commandments: "I am the Lord your God, who brought you out of the land of Egypt, out of the house of bondage. You shall have no other gods before me" (Exod. 20:2–3).

  - The book of Deuteronomy is written as a kind of sermon that Moses delivers to the Israelites before they enter the Promised Land. In it, Moses instructs the Israelites that once they are in the land of Canaan, they should break down the altars of the Canaanites and destroy their graven images (Deut. 7:5).

- The perspective we get on ancient Israelite religion in the Bible is one that is heavily controlled by the Deuteronomistic historians and the priests and scribes who compiled and edited the books of the Torah and the history of Israel.

- Nonetheless, in its critique of various religious practices, the Bible preserves accounts that document tremendous diversity in ancient Israelite religious practice.

Household Religion

- In a previous lecture, we discussed the household complex of Micah described in Judges 17–18. As we noted, Micah's household contained a family shrine, housed in its own structure in the extended family compound of Micah. The shrine contained several religious objects: a graven image, a molten image, an ephod, and teraphim.

  o The first two, graven and molten images, represent statues of divinities. In the story of Micah. they were poured and worked in silver. The Bible expressly forbids the making of this kind of image of a god. We don't know from the text of Judges whether these statues were meant to represent the Israelite god or two other gods. But the narrator offers no critique on this combining of religious accouterments.

  o An ephod, in most texts in the Bible, refers to a bejeweled garment worn by a priest, a tunic of sorts. In this text, it seems to be another statue or oracular device.

  o Teraphim are household gods, statues of gods that belong to a particular house.

- Micah's household shrine was tended by a priest. Initially, Micah's son fills this role, but then Micah replaces his son with a Levite, who becomes a paid member of Micah's house, with the specific responsibility of running the household shrine. Micah's response after hiring the priest indicates that priests were thought to bring the blessing of the Israelite god, even in a house shrine filled with statues of multiple divinities.

- In this story, the Israelite god, a Levite priest of Yahweh, a graven image, a molten image, an ephod, and some household gods all belong together. Micah, his family, and the Levite see no conflict with this combination of divinities. In fact, the combination is understood to be so powerful that the statues of the gods and the Levite are stolen from Micah when a band of men from the tribe of Dan happen upon the shrine.

Archaeological Evidence for Household Shrines

- Archaeological evidence for household shrines is sparse. This is due, in part, to archaeological practices that until recently did not carefully document where particular artifacts were found within common Israelite houses. This practice has now changed, and we are getting a much clearer picture of how various parts of the ancient Israelite house compound were used.

- It is not uncommon to find human-shaped and animal figurines in households, as well as objects that could be interpreted as serving religious functions. It is much rarer to find an actual room or structure within a house that can be identified as a household shrine.

- One example, however, is a household complex excavated in biblical Ai, dating to the premonarchic time period, around the 11th century B.C.E. This cluster of houses had one room that excavators identified as a shrine.
  - This room is significantly larger than other rooms in the compound and has stone benches built into the walls on two sides.

  - The contents of the room, including an offering stand, a large bowl, a chalice, animal figurines, and jewelry, indicate its special religious function. Some of these cult objects suggest food and drink offerings that may have been prepared and offered by women.

Israelite Worship of Ba'als and Asherim

- The Bible portrays Ba'al and Asherah, sometimes referred to in the singular and other times in the plural, as the god and goddess of the Canaanites. Nonetheless, we find both deities worshipped by ancient Israelites.

- In the royal household of the northern king Ahab of Israel, he and his Phoenician wife, Queen Jezebel, are said to dine with 450 prophets of Ba'al and 400 prophets of Asherah.

- The Bible repeatedly refers to "an Asherah" or plural "Asherim" as religious objects that Israelites and Judeans worshipped. These Asherim could be statues of the goddess, stylized trees that were associated with the goddess, or stone pillars, also associated with her worship.
  o Asherim were worshipped under trees and on mountains and hills but also, on several occasions, within the Jerusalem temple.

  o In 2 Kings 18, we read about the reign of King Hezekiah of Judah, a king judged as "good" by the Deuteronomistic historians. One of the actions he took that won him the favor of the Deuteronomists was removing the high places, breaking the pillars, and cutting down the Asherah.

Inscriptions from Kuntillet Ajrud
- In 1975–1976, archaeologists excavating at a site called Kuntillet Ajrud discovered a large collection of Hebrew inscriptions.
  o Kuntillet Ajrud is located in the Negev desert along a caravan route. It was not a developed village or city but probably a stopping point for travelers. Archaeologists have excavated a small fort there that was in use from around 850 to 750 B.C.E.

  o What makes this small site significant are inscriptions that include three references to people who are blessed in the name of "Yahweh and his Asherah."

  o The inscriptions were found on large pottery shards from broken jars, written by different scribes.

- Many of the inscriptions at Kuntillet Ajrud were labeled "letterheads" because they were pieces of correspondence in which a person was addressed with a blessing from a god or gods. The three referring to "Yahweh and his Asherah" are in this letterhead form.

- The inscriptions seem to attest to localized Yahwehs; there is a Yahweh of Samaria and a Yahweh of Teman. This localized understanding of a deity is found biblically in 2 Samuel 15:7 and in 1 Samuel 5:5.

- The mention of "his Asherah" allows for several interpretations. Perhaps they are to be understood as a pair of deities, that is, Yahweh and his consort, Asherah. Or the inscription may refer to the cult object of Asherah, a wooden pole or tree.

- The spelling of the personal names on the inscriptions points to people from the northern kingdom of Israel rather than Judah. The presence of a variety of scripts suggests that several different scribes or clerks were involved in writing. There were also some inscriptions written in the Phoenician script, suggesting the presence of travelers from this kingdom north of Israel, as well.

Judean Pillar Figurines

- Another type of archaeological object that may shed light on ancient Judean religious practices is what archaeologists have labeled Judean pillar figurines. These figurines date to the 8th and 7th centuries B.C.E., a century after the occupation dates of Kuntillet Ajrud.

- These objects are small, sculpted figurines of a humanlike female. They have round heads, and many have visible detail showing a headpiece or hairstyle. Their faces are sculpted with eyes and a nose, and sometimes, they have a mouth. Their bodies have pronounced, often disproportionately large breasts, and their hands are cupping and lifting their breasts.

- More than 1,000 of these pillar figurines have been unearthed in Judah. Interestingly almost half the finds have come from

Judean pillar figurines are often poorly made, suggesting that they were not luxury items; the clay used to make them likely came from the area around Jerusalem.

Jerusalem, the location of the temple and the priesthood. They are most often found in pillared houses, but they're also found in tombs and refuse piles.

- Scholars disagree about the functions of the figurines, but the most common theory is that they represent some sort of fertility or mother goddess, possibly the Canaanite goddess Asherah.
  - The link to Asherah in this theory is especially compelling. If their function is limited to fertility, it would be difficult to explain why we find the figures in tombs. Instead, they must have had a broader range of powers that were beneficial to both the living and the dead.

  - One factor that may work against these figures being a representation of the goddess Asherah is that they are often found broken in refuse heaps. If they were sacred objects, this seems an unlikely end for them.

  - Another weakness in this theory is that it does not specifically address the accentuated presence of breasts on these figurines. This feature has led several scholars to link them with healthy and abundant breastfeeding, although again, that interpretation would not explain their presence in tombs.

- We're left with more than 1,000 female figurines that are found in a relatively small geographic area and certainly had some sort of household function, one that probably continued to be beneficial to the dead. For whatever reason, the biblical writers did not find these objects threatening to the centralized worship of Yahweh in the Jerusalem temple because they do not mention or condemn them.

- Even when we don't have a clear answer as to what the figurines were, they help us to realize once again how diverse religious and household practices were and how much of ancient Judean and Israelite religion remains beyond our grasp.

Suggested Reading

Ackerman, "Household Religion," in Bodel and Olyan, eds., *Household and Family Religion in Antiquity*, pp. 126–158.

Dijkstra, "I Have Blessed You by YHWH of Samaria and His Asherah," in Becking et al., eds., *Only One God?*, pp. 16–44

Stavrakopoulou and Barton, eds., *Religious Diversity in Ancient Israel and Judah*, pp. 104–148.

Questions to Consider

1. How do the inscriptions found at Kuntillet Ajrud affect your understanding of ancient Israelite religion?

2. How is your understanding of biblical religion altered if Asherah was at one time Yahweh's consort?

3. Why do you think local worship practices continued even after the building of state sanctuaries?

Lives of the Rich, Lives of the Poor
Lecture 12

T his lecture brings our unit on kingdoms and king making to a close. We have seen how monarchic states developed gradually in ancient Israel and Judah. We've learned about the royal ideology that claimed divine sponsorship for kings. We've investigated the Jerusalem temple as a site of pilgrimage for average people and a site of economic power for the king. In this lecture, we will examine the beginnings of a socially stratified society during the time of the divided monarchy and the emergence of a new type of "rich" and a new type of "poor." We'll also see how village and family structures and ideals continued to exist, even as the monarchy grew more powerful.

Naboth's Vineyard
- The story of Naboth's Vineyard is set in the 9th century in the northern kingdom of Israel, during the reign of Ahab. The story is found in 1 Kings 21.

- In this story, we see the expansion of the royal palace's power and arrogance. The story begins with Ahab demanding that Naboth turn over his vineyard to be used for a vegetable garden; in exchange, Ahab offers either a better vineyard or cash. To an ancient hearer, several details of this story would seem appalling.
  o Because it takes years to mature, a vineyard was a valuable, long-term family investment. The idea that Ahab wants the vineyard for a vegetable garden would strike ancient hearers as wasteful, arrogant, and foolish.

  o Israel was also in the midst of a prolonged famine at this time, and despite this famine, Jezebel and Ahab regularly held lavish feasts.

  o Further, in ancient Israel, land was not considered an economic asset that one could buy and sell at will. The Israelite god owned the land and bestowed it upon a family to be cared for and passed down from father to son. Ahab's suggestion that he purchase family land with money portrays him as out of touch with the principles and values of the kinship-based society that Israel still was, in spite of the monarchy.

- As the story continues, the commoner, Naboth, reminds Ahab of the Israelite god's laws regarding ancestral land. Ahab returns home "resentful and sullen" (1 Kings 21:3–4).

- Jezebel, Ahab's queen, finds her husband with his face to the wall, refusing to eat, and asks him what's wrong. He relates the exchange with Naboth, and Jezebel promises that she will get him the vineyard.

- The story then shifts to a rapid description of the steps Jezebel takes to deliver Naboth's vineyard into the hands of Ahab. She writes letters in her husband's name to "the elders and the nobles who dwelt with Naboth," directing these men to accuse Naboth publically of cursing both God and king. They are then to stone Naboth for his crime.

- After her instructions are carried out and Naboth is dead, Jezebel tells Ahab to take possession of the vineyard.

Hallmarks of a State
- One of the marks of a fully developed state is a socially stratified society with clear demarcations between upper and lower classes.
  - An early state, such as that of Solomon or Jeroboam, is divided simply between ruler and ruled.

  - In a fully developed national state, people are divided into multiple classes that compete with one another for resources; the government sides with the upper class to secure its power over the one group that could potentially overthrow it.

- Another mark of a fully developed state is an increase in the size of the monarchy, shown through an increase in the number of titled royal officials. We have already noted such an increase in the movement from Saul to David to Solomon in the Bible.
  - o In this story of Ahab, nobles, governors of districts, a palace manager, and the queen all play significant roles in relationship to the monarchy's governance.

  - o The kinship-based authority entrusted to the elders continues even in the time of a fully developed monarchy, but as we see in this story, the elders now answer to the monarchy, even to the point of putting to death an innocent man of their own kin group.

- A third mark of a fully developed state is that the business of government is handled through written documents, evidenced here in the letters of Jezebel to the elders and nobles.

- It seems possible, then, to consider the dynasty of Omri as the first example of a fully developed state in ancient Israel. This seems a bit surprising because the northern kingdom had been marked by dynastic instability. But beginning with Omri, the Israelites enjoyed political stability for about 140 years.

Prophetic Critique of Amos
- By the 8th century, the northern kingdom of Israel was a fully stratified class society. We get a window into the nature of these class divisions in the writings of an 8th-century prophet named Amos.

- Amos is identified as a "seer" and as a "troubler of the king." He prophesied during the unusually long reign of Jeroboam II, in the first half of the 8th century B.C.E. This was a time when Assyria, the empire to the east, was weak, and Egypt was inactive in the region. Israel was independent, stable, and wealthy.

- We don't get much biographical information on Amos. He identifies himself by saying, "I am no prophet, nor a prophet's son; but I am a herdsman, and a dresser of sycamore trees" (Amos 7:14). The phrase "I am no prophet, nor a prophet's son" indicates that Amos does not belong to a prophetic guild. This seems to imply that he is not part of the royal household, and therefore, his prophetic word is truer.

- Many of Amos's prophecies come in the form of visions of doom and devastation for Israel in general and for the royal household in particular. Injustices related to the wealthy classes seem to be the main reason that the Israelite god will rain down punishments upon the kingdom.

- Amos's critique of the rich who prosper at the expense of the poor has had an enduring legacy. Many of his damning portrayals of the lives of the rich seem timeless.
    o For example, Amos has God testifying against the rich who own summer houses, winter houses, and ivory houses (Amos 3:13–15). The rich are those whose houses are made of hewn stone rather than the common baked mud brick. They sleep on beds of ivory and hold lavish feasts.

    o In both cases, Amos associates wealth and excess among the rich with their unjust behavior toward the poor. The rich are those who "trample upon the poor and take from them levies of grain"; they "take bribes" and "push aside the needy" (Amos 5:11–12).

- The people who are the poor and downtrodden in the book of Amos are distinct from the poor of the premonarchic and early monarchic periods.
    o In earlier times, the poor were those who fell outside the protective net of the kinship unit, such as widows and orphans, both of whom lacked the protection and provision of a male head of household. And they were resident aliens, what the Bible calls "sojourners," who could not claim automatic membership in a household.

o   In Amos's day, a new group had been added to "the poor": those who were in debt to the monarchy and to the landholding rich. This status was related to new taxes that were levied against all households, forcing them to contribute portions of their produce to the royal household.

Social Stratification and the Archaeological Record
- The social stratification that we begin to hear about in biblical texts and stories dating to the 8th century is reflected in the material culture of households and palaces.

- The palace at Samaria dates to the reigns of Omri and Ahab and has been excavated multiple times throughout the 20th century. It was built of finely hewn stone and had plastered floors. Such architectural features would have required a tremendous output of human labor.
  o   Excavations at the palace uncovered burned remains of incised ivory panels used to decorate furniture. Initially, this find was connected to the "ivory house" that Ahab is credited with building.

  o   More recent work on dating the ivory pieces, however, indicates that they were found in later settlement layers and likely date to the reign of Jeroboam II, the king who reigned during the time of Amos.

- Samaria also yielded a cache of more than 100 ostraca, inscribed potsherds similar to the ones found at Kuntillet Ajrud. Dating to the 8th century, these inscriptions record the payment of taxes in the form of produce.
  o   Some scholars argue that the Samaria ostraca document an elaborate, multi-tiered tax system whereby royal tax collectors, who may have been nobles and elders within their cities, collected taxes from a peasant class and delivered them to the palace, where the items were recorded.

- o Other scholars believe that the ostraca document a system of credit for wealthy landowners who had moved to the capital but still received financial backing from their landholding relatives back home.

- o Both scenarios move far away from the simple life of a man in a highland village who eats the produce of his own hands.

The Southern Kingdom of Judah

- Judah enjoyed greater political stability than its northern neighbor. It was ruled by the single dynasty of David for its entire history of more than 400 years.

- At the same time, as a smaller kingdom that was not in the heartland of what had been tribal Israel, the southern kingdom of Judah took a longer time to become a fully developed state.

Because of the corruption of the ruling officials in Jerusalem, Micah proclaims: "Zion shall be ploughed as a field [and] Jerusalem shall become a heap of ruins."

- In two 8th-century prophets operating in Judah, Isaiah of Jerusalem and Micah, we find critiques of prophets operating in the south that register the same class distinctions found in the north.
  - The same issues of oppression and the seizing of family estates that we saw in Amos appear in Micah 2:1–2. The passage almost seems to be written with Ahab in mind: "Alas for those who devise wickedness and evil deeds on their beds! ... They covet fields, and seize them; houses, and take them away; they oppress householder and house, a man and his inheritance."

  - Isaiah seems to have a similar type of land greediness in mind when he announces: "Ah, you who join house to house, who add field to field, until there is room for no one but you" (Isa. 5:8).

- The poor are likewise those who find themselves wrongfully in debt to the rich. Micah has God address those who "rise against my people as an enemy ... stripping the robes from the peaceful" (Mic. 2:8).

- Finally, Micah sees the corruption and greediness of those in power as the cause of Jerusalem's future destruction.

Suggested Reading

Dever, *The Lives of Ordinary People in Ancient Israel*, pp. 206–248.

Kessler, *The Social History of Ancient Israel*, pp. 103–117.

Questions to Consider

1. What was life like for a poor person in Israel during the monarchy?

2. How can a funny and exaggerated story, such as that of King Ahab and his wife, Jezebel, preserve genuine aspects of history?

3. According to the writings of Amos, Isaiah, and Micah, how did the rich live during the time of the monarchy?

Assyrian Incursion into Israel and Judah
Lecture 13

I n this lecture, we start a new unit on the age of empires. Historically, this unit encompasses the Assyrian and Babylonian empires that dominated the ancient Near East from the 9th through the 6th centuries B.C.E. In these lectures, we'll learn about Assyrian and Babylonian military tactics, witness the siege of Jerusalem, and examine the economic impact of heavy tributes required by Assyria and Babylonia. We'll also look at how Assyria's and Babylonia's differing policies of deportation led to the disappearance of the northern kingdom of Israel and the survival of the southern kingdom of Judah. This first lecture of the unit introduces the Neo-Assyrian Empire and covers the Assyrian conquest of the northern kingdom of Israel.

Overview of the Age of Empires
- The importance of the Assyrian Empire in the history of ancient Israel and Judah cannot be overstated.
    o From the earliest beginnings of the Assyrian Empire, its kings had an interest in controlling the kingdoms and territories of the west, where we find Israel and Judah, as well as Aram-Damascus, Tyre, Phoenicia, Philistia, Edom, Moab, and Ammon.

    o A recurrent boast found in Assyrian royal inscriptions is that the king of Assyria "washed his weapons" in the Mediterranean Sea. This boast indicated that the king had made it as far as the Mediterranean Sea, and along the way, he had slaughtered so many people that he needed to wash the blood off his weapons.

- Assyria's recorded history overlaps with the history preserved in the Bible at several key moments. For example, the Black Obelisk records Shalmaneser III's domination of several territories and his receipt of tribute from King Jehu of Israel.

The Neo-Assyrian Empire

- The Neo-Assyrian Empire dates from the 9th through the 7th centuries B.C.E. At its most expansive point, it controlled Mesopotamia, ancient Elam, Anatolia, and all of the Levant and briefly extended into Egypt. In modern terms, it encompassed the territory from western Iran to the Mediterranean Sea and from Turkey to Egypt.

- Several features mark the political and national entity of Assyria as an empire.
  - The backbone of political control was the military, and the primary role of the king was to lead his army into battle. Royal texts present the kings as warriors who fight on behalf of the Assyrian national god, Assur.

  - Assyria not only conquered foreign nations, but it established an administrative apparatus that enabled it to maintain control of its conquests. Assyrian-appointed governors ruled in conquered territories, and conquered foreign kings were forced to swear loyalty to their Assyrian overlords and pledge annual tribute. Conquered peoples were deported to far-flung territories of the empire, and conquered armies were absorbed into the Assyrian fighting force.

  - Another feature that marks Assyria as an empire is monumental building. Almost every successive king founded his own capital city, built a palace, and built or refurbished temples. Conquered people provided the labor for these building projects, and wealth forcibly extracted through tribute provided the funding.

  - Writing and recordkeeping are also important marks of imperial rule. In the Assyrian Empire, scribes, writing the Akkadian language in cuneiform script, kept records of the kings' activities and correspondence. These written texts, along with inscribed stone monuments, provide us with a richness of source material that we do not have for any of the previous periods of Israelite and Judean history.

- One example of the richness of source material for this period is found in the reign of the Assyrian king Tiglath-Pileser III.
  - This king reigned from 745 to 727 B.C.E.; his reign marked the resurgence of the Assyrian Empire's active domination of the kingdoms of the Levant.

  - We know of Tiglath-Pileser III from multiple sources, including his royal inscriptions and his palace reliefs, which depict him laying siege to an unnamed enemy city.

  - The Israelites also knew of Tiglath-Pileser III. The Bible refers to him more than once, calling him King Pul of Assyria. And it is under this king that both Israel and Judah became vassals of Assyria.

Israel as a Vassal State

- In 2 Kings 15, we find an account of the reign of Menahem in the northern kingdom of Israel. The text tells us that Menahem paid tribute to Pul to "confirm his hold of royal power." This indicates that Menahem saw Tiglath-Pileser III as a potential ally who could help him secure his kingship at home.

© David Castor/Wikimedia Commons/Public Domain.

Palace reliefs were meant to communicate the absolute power of the Assyrian king.

- We then learn that Menahem exacted this tribute money for Assyria from the "wealthy families" in Israel. Already in this early stage of imperial domination, we see the royal payment of an imperial tribute becoming a burdensome domestic tax.

- As we said earlier, the relative wealth that Israel began to amass during the Omride dynasty would now be redirected to Assyria as tribute, and Israel would remain a vassal to Assyria until its conquest by that same empire in 722 B.C.E.

The Situation in Judah

- In 734, Tiglath-Pileser III returned to the kingdoms of the Levant to reassert his control. According to the Bible, the king of Israel, Pekah, formed a coalition with Rezin of Aram-Damascus to resist Tiglath-Pileser's advance. In other words, the vassal state of Israel planned to rebel against Assyria to regain its independent status.

- Pekah and Rezin then turned to King Ahaz of Judah to ask him to join in the rebellion. At this point, Judah was not a vassal of Assyria. When King Ahaz declined, Rezin and Pekah attacked him in Jerusalem in an effort to depose Ahaz and force Judah to join the coalition.

- Ahaz, however, sent to Tiglath-Pileser III for help against Israel and Aram. The biblical record of this request has King Ahaz use the language of a vassal treaty to subject himself to the king of Assyria in return for Tiglath-Pileser's protection against Israel (2 Kings 16:7).

- The rebellion failed, and Israel and Aram-Damascus remained tribute-paying vassals. This story is a classic example of how imperial power works by pitting smaller local kingdoms against each other. In this case, Judah became a vassal to protect itself from Israel. The house of Jacob was truly divided in this historical moment.

The Conquest of Israel

- In 722 B.C.E., after only two decades under Assyrian domination, the northern kingdom of Israel was conquered and its capital of Samaria was destroyed by Sargon II. His own record of the event reads: "The city of Samaria I besieged and I conquered … 27,290 people who resided in it I took as booty. I conscripted fifty chariots from them and the rest I had instructed in their proper behavior. My eunuch I appointed over them, and I imposed on them the tribute like the previous king."

- The Bible's record of this event in 2 Kings 17 is a good example of the Deuteronomistic historians' presentation of source material.
  - After a standard introduction, we read repeated references to written material taken from the "annals" of the kings of Israel and Judah. Although we have recovered no such texts, the Deuteronomists' citation of these materials suggests that the information they contained was specific to each king, rather than formulaic summaries.

  - Interestingly, the historical report on the conquest of the northern kingdom of Israel is related in only two short verses (2 Kings 17:5–6), and again, this material likely comes from one of the Deuteronomistic historians' written sources. Clearly, the historians' interests lie not in describing the three-year siege of Samaria but in relating why the conquest occurred: "because the people of Israel had sinned against the Lord their God" (2 Kings 17:7).

- From the Deuteronomists' record of the conquest, we learn that the Assyrian king deported the Israelites to multiple places in his empire. Historians estimate that tens of thousands of Israelites were deported, and then, as was standard Assyrian practice, countless other conquered peoples were forcibly settled in the conquered territory of Israel.
  - This policy of scattering conquered populations and resettling conquered lands with other exiled populations was designed

to disrupt national identity and reduce the chances for national rebellions.

o The effectiveness of the policy is confirmed by our current reference to the tribes of the northern kingdom as the "lost tribes of Israel."

Implications of a Second Exile

- In an earlier lecture, we looked at a nonlinear timeline; the Babylonian Exile was placed at the center of this timeline as a critical time period for the compilation and editing of what would eventually become the Bible. At this point in the course, we know that ancient Israel and Judah actually experienced two conquests and exiles, and both had implications for the ultimate shape of the Bible.

- After the conquest of Samaria, some of the northern Israelites must have moved south, because the Bible, compiled and preserved by Judeans, tells the stories of the north. These northern stories are told from a distinctly Judean perspective, but we can still find stories that had their origins in the north.
  - o The Deuteronomistic history was compiled and edited during the 100 or so years just after the fall of northern Israel and leading up to the fall of Judah. One of the central beliefs of the Deuteronomistic historians is that the division of the united kingdom of David into two kingdoms was a mistake and that the divinely anointed dynasty that would endure was that of David.

  - o These historians used an interesting literary structure to communicate the intended unity of the northern and southern kingdoms of Israel and Judah. They interleaved the histories of the two kingdoms together, moving back and forth from north to south. This literary pattern communicates the idea that there is one history of Israel and one nation of Israel, and the divinely appointed royal house over "all Israel" is that of David.

○ This southern viewpoint will lay the groundwork for Judah, the one remaining tribe, to take on the mantle of "all Israel" during the Babylonian Exile.

Stresses of Assyrian Domination

- The period of Assyrian domination over Israel and Judah created multiple stress points in both kingdoms.

- First, there were political costs. In Israel, we find tremendous political instability during the Assyrian period, and there were political costs in the relationship between Israel and Judah. Political friction and gamesmanship resulted in Israel attacking Jerusalem and Judah calling in Assyria as an ally against Israel.

- We can also document economic costs—significant hardship related to paying tribute to Assyria.

- Finally, there were significant social costs. We see the breakup of family and village life as sons were required to fight battles and wealth was exacted from villages to the crown to pay ever-growing burdens of tribute and taxes to Assyria.

- Once Israel was conquered and deported, each of these stress points only increased for Judah as it continued to struggle with Assyrian control.

Suggested Reading

Dever, *The Lives of Ordinary People in Ancient Israel*, pp. 320–344.

Mieroop, *A History of the Ancient Near East, ca. 3000–323 BC*, pp. 216–252.

1. How do images of Assyrian warfare alter your perspective on biblical history?

2. What were the political and military objectives of the Assyrian deportation policy that involved scattering conquered peoples and resettling their land with other conquered peoples?

Life under Siege
Lecture 14

With the conquest of the northern kingdom of Israel, our attention shifts by default to the southern kingdom of Judah, the kingdom that will become the memory holder for "all Israel." We will devote this lecture to a single transformative encounter between Judah and Assyria: Sennacherib's siege of Jerusalem in 701 B.C.E. How did the ancient Judeans view the Assyrians? Were they able to place them in one of their existing categories of enemies, or did this new empire require new language? And what was it like to live in a city under siege? In this lecture, we'll focus on this particularly important moment in the history of Judah to provide detailed answers to these questions.

The Reign of King Hezekiah

- King Hezekiah ruled Judah beginning in the late 8th century and continuing through the beginning of the 7th century. He ascended the throne of Judah at about the time of Assyria's conquest of the northern kingdom of Israel. His story is told in 2 Kings 18–20, 2 Chronicles 29–32, and Isaiah 36–39. Although Hezekiah ruled for close to three decades, the biblical account focuses on only three events: his religious reform, his military encounter with Sennacherib, and his illness.

- From the multiple accounts in the Bible and the archaeological record, we're able to piece together a more complete picture of Hezekiah's reign.
    - Judah escaped any direct impact from Assyria during its campaign against Israel. During the first decade of Hezekiah's reign, he remained a loyal vassal to Assyria; as a result, Judah enjoyed considerable economic prosperity.

    - Hezekiah embarked on a religious reform that removed outlying shrines, referred to as "high places." He broke the sacred poles and cut down the Asherim.

o Archaeological surveys of the Judean hill country show that under Hezekiah, many new settlements were established and the developed area of the capital city of Jerusalem was expanded. The most logical explanation for these new settlements is that some of the northern Israelites escaped deportation and fled south to Judah. Again, this explains how we get northern Israel's history preserved in southern Judah's Bible.

o The biblical account of Hezekiah's reign that begins in 2 Kings 18 spends little time describing this decade of prosperity. Instead, it moves almost immediately to Hezekiah's military encounter with Assyria (2 Kings 18:7). Although this might suggest that Hezekiah's rebellion occurred almost from the beginning of his reign, it is likely to have occurred after the death of Sargon II in 705, when Assyria was seen to be weak.

• As a result of Hezekiah's rebellion, Sennacherib comes to Judah to reassert his control. Hezekiah sends a message to the king of Assyria at Lachish, saying, "'I have done wrong; withdraw from me; whatever you impose on me I will bear'" (2 Kings 18:13–14).

• The biblical account does not stress Hezekiah's military preparedness for an attack, but the archaeological record suggests that he anticipated a siege on Jerusalem.
  o An excavated city wall on the western side of Jerusalem suggests that Hezekiah had fortified the walls of the city in anticipation of an Assyrian attack.

  o Hezekiah also completed the Siloam tunnel, which would supply water to the city from the Gihon spring.

  o In addition, evidence in the form of hundreds of royally stamped storage jars suggests that Hezekiah stockpiled provisions of oil and grain in preparation for a long siege.

The Horrors of Siege
- Even before Sennacherib arrived in Judah, it's likely that Judeans had an idea of the horrors associated with living in a city under siege. These horrors would form the basis for an Assyrian campaign of psychological warfare that would encourage soldiers and villagers alike to surrender without a fight.
  - The standard language of cursing included references to siege. Deuteronomy, for example, closes its covenantal section with a series of curses uttered against anyone "who does not obey the voice of the Lord your God" (Deut. 28:15). Among the many horrible fates that will befall this disobedient person, we read, "In the desperate straits to which the enemy siege reduces you, you will eat the fruit of your womb, the flesh of your own sons and daughters" (Deut. 28:53).

  - When the biblical character Job is in the midst of his greatest distress, having lost everything, he imagines that God has walled up his way and broken him down on every side. He tells his friends that the troops of God have "thrown up siege-works" against him (Job 19:8–12).

- The Judeans' actual experience with Assyria would also lead to dread. The prophet Isaiah describes the army of the nation that would conquer Israel: "Their arrows are sharp, all their bows bent, their horses' hoofs seem like flint and their wheels like the whirlwind. Their roaring is like a lion" (Isa. 5:28–29). This description closely matches the Assyrians' own carefully crafted self-image carved onto the walls of their palaces.

Sennacherib's Campaign against Judah
- To avoid an immediate attack by Sennacherib, the biblical account indicates that Hezekiah paid a tribute of silver and gold that he had stripped from the temple and palace.

- Sennacherib then sent two of his officials, the Rabsaris and the Rab Shakeh, to Jerusalem. Hezekiah sends his representatives to meet with Sennacherib's officials.

- The officials read aloud a letter from Sennacherib. The letter is a skillfully crafted piece of propaganda meant as much for the inhabitants of Jerusalem as it is for Hezekiah. Sennacherib asks Hezekiah about the source of his confidence for rebelling against Assyria. He then lists and refutes all the likely arguments circulating in Jerusalem about how Judah might triumph over Assyria.

- Hezekiah's palace representatives immediately realize the danger of the Rab Shakeh's words, and they beg him to speak in Aramaic, a diplomatic language not understood by the citizens of the city. But the Rab Shakeh then directly addresses the residents of Jerusalem in their own language. He warns them about the horrors of a siege but promises that by making peace with Sennacherib, they can enjoy prosperity, safety, and stability.

Biblical Version of Sennacherib's Attack

- In trying to determine what actually happened in Sennacherib's campaign, we must examine multiple accounts. Our sources include the Bible, Sennacherib's royal inscriptions and carved wall panels in his palace, and the Babylonian Chronicles. Remarkably, these sources agree on several details:
  - Jerusalem was not destroyed. Sennacherib and his forces did not enter Jerusalem.

  - Sennacherib returned to Assyria shortly after conquering the cities of Judah, including Lachish.

  - Hezekiah paid heavy tribute to Sennacherib.

  - Sennacherib was murdered by his own sons.

- The biblical version of the story credits the Israelite god with the survival of Jerusalem.
  - In two trips to the temple, Isaiah tells Hezekiah that Sennacherib will not succeed against Jerusalem. In the second trip, the Lord's answer to Hezekiah is given in the form of a

poem in which Jerusalem is personified as a woman, "Daughter Zion," who mocks the king of Assyria.

- o We then hear directly from the Israelite god that the Assyrian king is merely a tool in his hands.

- o The biblical record concludes with the retreat and death of Sennacherib. An angel of the Lord strikes down 185,000 Assyrian soldiers in one night, and when Sennacherib sees the bodies, he returns to his home in Nineveh. The next verse tells us that he was killed by his own sons.

- The biblical record suggests that the Israelite god is in charge of history. This national god is able to command foreign kings, call up foreign armies, and deliver a punishment against his people but, ultimately, save a remnant of them and protect his city. The Assyrian king is reduced to nothing more than a pawn. He is forced to flee and is killed by his sons in the temple of his own ineffectual god.

Assyrian Version of Sennacherib's Attack
- Sennacherib's record of his campaign against Judah is much shorter because it's just one part a larger military victory against the west. He claims to have besieged 46 of Hezekiah's walled cities, including Jerusalem, but he does not claim to have conquered and destroyed Jerusalem. Nor does he suggest that he fled Jerusalem in fear.

- The campaign against Judah receives detailed attention in the visual narrative found in Sennacherib's palace at Nineveh.
  - o The siege of Lachish is covered in several panels. In one depiction, the Assyrian forces have entered the city and are battling with Judean soldiers, most of whom are surrendering. The hillsides outside the city are built up with siege ramps, and advancing up the ramps are multiple battering rams.

  - o A second set of panels shows an aerial view of the occupation of the city by the Assyrian king and his forces. Sennacherib sits

Just as Isaiah described them, the Assyrian soldiers shown at Nineveh are not weary; they do not stumble; and their bows are taut.

enthroned within the walls of Lachish, and conquered Judean men bow before him.

o A final set of panels shows the deportation of the inhabitants of Lachish.

- Clearly, Lachish was the visual icon of Sennacherib's Judean campaign. Visitors to the palace couldn't help but be impressed by these scenes depicting the siege, conquest, and deportation of Lachish. Such visitors would not know that Lachish was not the capital city and would probably conclude that Judah had been conquered by Sennacherib.

Conflicting Accounts
- Both the biblical and the Assyrian records of this military encounter record a victory.
  o The Bible records a victory for the Israelite god, who successfully punishes his people by bringing the Assyrians

against them. At the same time, he preserves a remnant and protects his city of Jerusalem. Ultimately, he teaches the Assyrian king a lesson, killing thousands of his troops, sending him back to his own land, and possibly even orchestrating his murder at the hands of his sons.

o The Assyrian sources record a victory for Sennacherib, who destroys countless fortified cities, exacts heavy tributes, and deports the inhabitants of the conquered cities. Instead of fleeing the angel of death sent by the Israelite god, Sennacherib leaves Judah, having received the tribute he wanted from Hezekiah. And as it turns out, his death comes years later, not immediately.

- The survival of Jerusalem and, therefore, Judah has profound implications for the history of Israel and the formation of the Bible.
  o If Judah had been completely conquered by the Assyrians, the Judeans would have been scattered in exile, as the Israelites from the north had been. They would have become yet another "lost tribe."

  o Instead, likely because Hezekiah agreed to pay a heavier tribute and remain a loyal vassal, Judah survived, and with its survival, the stories of the Bible continued to take shape and get passed down to succeeding generations.

Suggested Reading

Carr, *An Introduction to the Old Testament*, pp. 131–164.

Chapman, *The Gendered Language of Warfare in the Israelite-Assyrian Encounter*, pp. 20–111.

Machinist, "The Rab Sāqêh at the Wall of Jerusalem."

1. In what ways did common Judeans experience Assyria's efforts at psychological warfare?

2. What aspects of Judah's religious beliefs are challenged by the military encounter with Assyria?

3. How can we account for the Rab Shakeh's detailed knowledge of Judean language and internal disputes?

Religious Debates and Preserved Text
Lecture 15

In our last lecture, we discussed Jerusalem's survival of Sennacherib's attack on Judah in 701 B.C.E. After Sennacherib left the region, Judah existed for another 115 years, outlasting the Assyrian Empire, which was conquered by Babylonia in 612 B.C.E. Babylonia asserted its control over the same regions as Assyria had; thus, the situation for Judah under Babylonia was not significantly different. Ultimately, King Nebuchadrezzar conquered Judah in two campaigns. His destruction of Jerusalem in 586 B.C.E. marked the beginning of the Babylonian Exile. Before we turn to the exile, however, we will use this lecture to focus on two critical areas of development: the religious debates that characterized the 7th century and the formation of the Deuteronomistic history.

Religious Debates and Reforms

- The biblical record of the 7th century attests to a multiplicity of religious practices observed by kings and commoners alike.

- Among the kings, Manasseh (r. 698/697–642 B.C.E.) stands out as one that the Deuteronomistic historians judge for his worship of foreign gods.
    - Manasseh ascended the throne after Hezekiah's death and reigned for a remarkable 55 years (2 Kings 21:1).

    - The Deuteronomists accuse Manasseh of rebuilding the high places that Hezekiah had destroyed, erecting altars to Ba'al and other deities, and even practicing child sacrifice.

- As we saw in the last lecture, in his speech on the wall of Jerusalem, Rab Shakeh had sought to divide the Judeans using their differing views of Hezekiah's reform.
    - Hezekiah had destroyed the outlying shrines, cut down the Asherim, and removed foreign idols from the Jerusalem temple.

o The Rab Shakeh reminded the common people that these actions by their king forced them to worship only in Jerusalem.

- This line of argument suggests a real division among the Judeans concerning the centralization of worship in the Jerusalem temple.
  o Clearly, some Judeans saw their local shrines or high places as legitimate places of worship, where they could offer sacrifices to the Israelite god.

  o It also seems likely that many Judeans saw no conflict between worshipping the Israelite god and worshipping Ba'al, Asherah, and the astral deities associated with the sun, moon, and stars.

  o It is possible, therefore, to imagine that some segments of the Judean population supported Manasseh's rebuilding of the high places and rededication of altars to Ba'al and Asherah. Given that Judah had been held in desperate economic straights and in fear for its survival by the Assyrians and the Babylonians, it seems likely that the Judeans turned to whichever gods they thought might protect them. It also seems natural that in a time of crisis, there would be multiple factions that disagreed with one another about the proper form of worship.

The Reform of Josiah (r. 640–609 B.C.E.)

- After Manasseh's death and a very brief reign of Amon, Josiah ascended the throne in Judah as a boy king; he succeeded in ruling Judah for 31 years. The Deuteronomists remember Josiah as one who "did right in the eyes of the Lord" (2 Kings 22:2).

- The biblical record of Josiah's reign is found in 2 Kings 22–23.
  o There, we read that Josiah had financed the repair of the temple in Jerusalem. While the repair was underway, Hilkiah, the high priest of the temple, reported, "I have found the book of the law in the house of the Lord" (2 Kings 22:8).

  o The king's secretary, Shaphan, reads the book to Josiah, and as soon as Josiah hears the words, he realizes that he and the inhabitants of Judah have not been living according to the laws in this book.

- o The king then seeks out the advice of a prophetess named Huldah. She predicts that great evil will come upon the land because the people have not obeyed the words of the book and have instead worshipped other gods.

- o After hearing the words of Huldah, Josiah gathered all the people at the Jerusalem temple to read aloud from the book. He then made a covenant with his god in front of all the people, promising to "follow the Lord … [and] to perform the words of this covenant that were written in this book."

Josiah's use of the "book of the law" is one of our first examples of a book functioning as authoritative scripture.

- The resulting reform carried out by Josiah was sweeping and violent—even deadly. The main goal of the reform was to centralize worship of the Israelite god in the Jerusalem temple alone.
  - To accomplish this goal, Josiah purged the Jerusalem temple of all cultic items related to the worship of other gods, including vessels made for Ba'al, Asherah, and the Assyrian astral deities.

  - The rival northern altar at Bethel, first erected by Jeroboam I, was singled out for special treatment. Josiah tore down the altar and burned the temple there. He unearthed bodies that had been buried near the temple, placed the bones on the destroyed altar, and burned them to fully defile the space.

  - Josiah then destroyed all the smaller shrine sites throughout Samaria and slaughtered their priests.

- Although the Bible's perspective is that the Israelites should worship only one god, these repeated efforts at religious reform show that Judeans continued to worship many gods in many places. Based on what Josiah destroyed, we can conclude that Judeans burned incense and made offerings to Ba'al, a sun god, and the gods of Sidon, Moab, and Ammon. Judean women wove cloth for Asherah. Parents sacrificed their children to a god called Molech. Judeans worshipped these gods in the Jerusalem temple, in local shrines, at city gates, in valleys, and on rooftops.

- From the language associated with the book and the reforms enacted based on it, scholars have associated it with some form of Deuteronomy. This is the final book of the Torah, in which Moses provides instructions for the Israelites who are about to enter the Promised Land. The book of Deuteronomy is appropriately labeled a "book of the law of Moses."

- The history of the monarchy described in 1 and 2 Kings reveals an ongoing royal and priestly struggle to control Judean religious practices.

- o In three generations of Judean kings, we see Hezekiah eliminate outlying shrines, Manasseh rebuilding them, and Josiah tearing them down again.

- o Although there is no question that the Deuteronomistic historians are presenting history with a bias toward the single god–single temple viewpoint, this back-and-forth struggle likely reflects a genuine historical debate among Judeans.

- o Josiah's reform, even though it is presented as sweeping and definitive, did not resolve the debate.

Worship of the Queen of Heaven

- During the last 23 years of Judah's history, four kings would reign, each one trying desperately to find the right policy for survival under Babylonian rule. When Judah and Jerusalem ultimately did fall to Babylonia in 586 B.C.E., we find one more example of ongoing religious debates among Judeans.

- Jeremiah was a prophet from the late 7th through the early 6th centuries B.C.E. He witnessed the conquest of Jerusalem by the Babylonians, and he remained in Jerusalem for a time after the conquest. Eventually, he was exiled to Egypt with a community of Judeans.

- We hear about a goddess known as the Queen of Heaven in two texts of Jeremiah that condemn her worship. In the first of these texts, Jeremiah announces the Israelite god's judgment on the families who engage in this worship (Jer. 7:17–18).
  - o This brief text paints a picture of common household religion that engages the whole family in preparing offerings to the Queen of Heaven and other unnamed deities.

  - o Jeremiah highlights this practice in order to ridicule it and pronounce judgment against those who engage in this kind of worship.

- The second mention of the Queen of Heaven is near the end of the book of Jeremiah, in chapter 44.
  - When Jerusalem fell to the Babylonians, Jeremiah was one of the leading prophetic voices that explained this conquest as the result of the people's sinfulness. In his view, the Judeans had broken the covenant with the Israelite god and worshiped other gods; as a result, their own god vacated his city and allowed the Babylonians to conquer it. This theological explanation of the conquest proved powerful and enduring.

  - Jeremiah 44 begins with a divine oracle of judgment upon the Judeans who have been exiled to Egypt. Here, the Israelite god claims responsibility for the conquest of Jerusalem. He brought the Babylonians to punish the Judeans for their wickedness.

  - The Israelite god then says that he sent prophets to the people to try to convince them to stop burning incense to idols and worshipping gods that their ancestors would not recognize. But the people, according to Jeremiah, did not listen to him or to any previous prophet; thus, the Israelite god "poured forth his wrath" in "the cities of Judah and the streets of Jerusalem."

  - When Jeremiah gets specific about what he means by the "wickedness" the people had committed, he first makes it clear that his judgment includes common men and women. He then indicates that the wickedness consists of burning incense to idols, and because of this practice, all the Judeans in Egypt will become "an execration, a horror, a curse, and a taunt."

  - Interestingly, Jeremiah's account preserves the people's response to his words. They reject his view of how and why the conquests of Jerusalem and Judah occurred and vow to continue worshipping the Queen of Heaven. They assert that this worship is an authentic Judean religious practice that has brought prosperity in the past. In fact, they blame the fall of Judah on such people as Jeremiah, who insisted on discontinuing worship of the Queen of Heaven.

Religious Reform and Biblical Text

- Throughout the period of Assyrian and then Babylonian domination of Judah, Judeans engaged in a diversity of religious practices as they sought to find security in the midst of constant foreign threats.

- The Bible preserves a debate within the Judean community concerning what constitutes authentic Judean religious practices, and this debate took on added urgency once the very survival of the nation was at stake.

- Ultimately, those who compiled and edited the biblical narrative were the priests and scribes who advocated the exclusive worship of the Israelite god. But they managed to preserve enough of the counter-narrative in the stories of Manasseh and the Judean exiles in Egypt that we have a fuller understanding of what kinds of beliefs and practices prevailed among royalty and commoners alike.

Suggested Reading

Ackerman, "At Home with the Goddess," in Dever and Gitin, eds., *Symbiosis, Symbolism, and the Power of the Past*, pp. 455–468.

Stavrakopoulou and Barton, *Religious Diversity in Ancient Israel and Judah*.

Questions to Consider

1. Why do you think a military crisis with Babylonia led to religious strife and disagreements within the Judean community?

2. What political purposes were served by Manasseh's policy of rebuilding outlying shrines and allowing the worship of multiple deities?

3. Why do you think Judeans might have been drawn to the worship of the Queen of Heaven?

Ezekiel—Exilic Informant
Lecture 16

A
lthough we tend to focus on 586 B.C.E., the date of the fall of Jerusalem, the Babylonian conquest of Jerusalem actually took place in stages. Ten years earlier, in 597, Nebuchadrezzar had removed the king of Jerusalem from the throne and deported the elite to Babylonia. In 588, Nebuchadrezzar returned to Jerusalem in response to a rebellion and laid siege to the city for two years. He then sent another group of Judeans into exile. A large portion of this group was taken to Babylonia, where they were settled together in a few cities. In this lecture, we will focus on Ezekiel, an eyewitness to the Babylonian conquest and a first-person informant on the experience of exile.

Ezekiel the Prophet

- The book of Ezekiel begins by introducing Ezekiel as "a priest" (Ezek. 1:3); it also signals that he is a prophet when it claims that Ezekiel saw "visions of God" and that the "word of the Lord came to him" (Ezek. 1:1–3).

- Ezekiel's prophetic career spanned 30 years, from 593 to 563 B.C.E. According to his own report, he was part of the first deportation of Judean elites to Babylonia in 597 B.C.E., and it was in Babylonia that he first began to have visions and speak the prophetic word.

- The book of Ezekiel contains many oracles and pronouncements that likely go back to the prophet himself, but it also clearly contains material that postdates the prophet. In general, the book can be divided into three historical periods, each defined by a central concern.
  - Chapters 1–24 contain a series of warnings concerning the disaster that is about to befall Jerusalem. These can be dated between 593 and 586 B.C.E.

- o Chapters 25–32 contain a series of judgments against the nations directly involved in Judah's conquest or those that stood by or celebrated Judah's conquest.

- o Chapters 33–48 contain visions of hope and restoration for the people of Judah in their homeland, complete with a rebuilt temple.

Ezekiel as Exilic Informant

- Ezekiel's life story and his visions and symbolic actions provide a rare glimpse of what life was like for a Judean who experienced military conquest and exile. Although Ezekiel was a priest and a member of the Jerusalem elite, much of what he experienced and prophesied about applied to the lives of all Judeans who experienced the Babylonian conquest.

- Ezekiel's own experiences of devastation and personal loss mirror those of the nation he hoped to restore. In the fifth year of his exile in Babylonia, he began to see visions of the Israelite god and to hear oracles that he was to deliver to the "house of Israel." The visions he experienced during his time in exile, prior to the actual fall of Jerusalem, are permeated with violence, depravation, death, and destruction.

- From the very beginning, Ezekiel's prophetic task is tied up with his personal life. He is struck mute by God, but his incapacity to speak is selective and purposeful.
  - o God tells Ezekiel that he will make the prophet's tongue cleave to the roof of his mouth so that Ezekiel will be unable to warn what God considers to be the rebellious, unrepentant house of Israel (Ezek. 3:22–27).

  - o But he will not be completely unable to speak: The Israelite god will loose his tongue to enable him to speak oracles of doom against Judah and Jerusalem.

- o Ezekiel's selective muteness lasts for about seven years, until he receives word that Jerusalem has fallen.

- o Although Ezekiel's muteness serves a clear theological purpose in the book, it also likely describes the experiences of trauma that many of the exiles had when they lost loved ones in the battle with Babylonia and were forcibly led from their homes to a foreign land.

- Ezekiel also loses his wife while in exile and is told by God that he may not observe the customary mourning rites for her (Ezek. 24:16–17).
  - o Again, Ezekiel's personal experience of the loss of his wife becomes a symbol for the entire nation's loss of many loved ones.

  - o When Ezekiel explains to the exiles why he is not observing the mourning rites for his wife, he tells them that God is preparing to destroy his sanctuary, and in that destruction, the exiles' sons and daughters—those they were forced to leave behind—will fall by the sword. Those who are already in exile, when they hear the news of the deaths of their children, will not be allowed to mourn for them.

- Ezekiel also engages in a series of sign acts, what we might call today performance art. He physically enacts what siege, conquest, and deportation will mean for his people.
  - o Every action of Ezekiel's life becomes a sign for the people of the devastation that will come to Jerusalem when it finally falls to Babylonia.

  - o Ezekiel knows the trauma of physical dislocation and loss of loved ones, the fear and deprivation that come with military siege, and the scenes of horror viewed by survivors as they are led out of a conquered city and into an unknown land.

The Valley of Dry Bones
- We have not recovered carved images of siege and deportation from Babylonia like the ones found in abundance from the palaces of the Assyrians. Still, the devastation that Judean exiles would have witnessed as they were marched from their cities would be similar to that depicted by the Assyrians.
  - Piles of corpses, many dismembered and mutilated, would be scattered in the streets, on the city walls, and outside the city.

  - Not being able to bury their loved ones would have added to the experience of trauma and loss the exiles experienced as they were led out of their devastated cities.

  - Thus, it is not surprising that Ezekiel focuses on issues of inability to mourn, inability to speak, and inability to bury one's dead.

- Throughout the Bible, the lack of a proper burial constitutes a curse and a punishment. In the book of Deuteronomy, one of the curses that will befall anyone who does not obey the statutes of the covenant involves military conquest and death without burial (Deut. 28:26). Deuteronomy describes a scene that would have been similar to what the Judeans confronted as they marched out of their fallen cities.

- To understand how the exiles would have felt leaving their dead unburied, we need to know something about Judean burial practices during normal times and the beliefs concerning an afterlife.
  - Ancient Israelites and Judeans did not have a concept of heaven and hell. Instead, those who died were thought to be in a kind of sleep. The place for the dead was called Sheol, but this was not an active place like heaven or hell. It was imagined as an underworld, often called "the pit."

  - People were buried in family tombs, usually caves, that were laid out in a similar manner to the pillared houses. Burials were often a two-staged process. In the first stage, the corpse was laid out on a bench in the family tomb, where it was left to decompose. Later, family members would return, gather the bones, and place them in a pit or repository in the floor of the cave, where they would rest with the bones of earlier ancestors.

o   Artifacts found within these burial caves, including animal bones, serving vessels, tools, weapons, and jewelry, suggest some concept of an afterlife.

•   Ezekiel's many visions of death and destruction clearly spoke to a central concern of the exiles: What had happened to the love ones left unburied in Judah? To answer this question, we turn to another section of the book of Ezekiel, the section focused on restoration. Here, we find the famous vision of the valley of dry bones.

o   In chapter 37, the Israelite god drops Ezekiel into a valley filled with dry bones. On one level, these exposed bones are precisely the image that has haunted the exiles as they think of those in Judah whom they had to leave unburied. On another level, however, the bones are a metaphor for the exiles themselves, who have lost hope of ever returning to their homeland.

o   In the vision, God asks Ezekiel, "Can these bones live?" Ezekiel answers, "Only you know." The bones are then brought to life (Ezek. 37:10).

Ezekiel prophesies to the dry bones, which then come together to form skeletons; flesh and sinews grow over the bones, and finally, God commands the wind to breathe into them.

o   This living, breathing host is meant to give

hope to the exiles that they will live again as a mighty nation in their own land, but it also begins to articulate a change in the views of the afterlife that occurred during and after the exile. By the 2nd century B.C.E., some segments of the Judean population had developed a belief in the resurrection of the dead.

Theological Developments in Response to Exile

- As we saw at the beginning of the course, in Psalm 137, captive Judeans asked: How can we sing the Lord's song in a land that is not our own? After the conquest of the northern kingdom and, again, after the conquest of the southern kingdom, they asked: If our god is all powerful, and we are his chosen, covenantal people, why didn't our god protect us from our enemies? Ezekiel's visions provide answers.

- In the opening vision of the book of Ezekiel, the prophet sits among the exiles by the river Chebar and receives a visitation from the Israelite god, enthroned on a winged, wheeled chariot.
  - o In the face of conquest and destruction, this first vision communicates the idea that the Israelite god has become mobile. The fact that he appears to Ezekiel in exile is evidence that this is a god who can travel.

  - o Thus, the exiles' first question is partially answered: They can sing the Lord's song in a different land because the Lord is present with them in exile.

- Ezekiel's answer to the second question comes in chapter 8 of his book. This vision is dated to 592, before the final conquest of Jerusalem.
  - o Here, God shows Ezekiel Israelites engaged in foreign worship practices in the Jerusalem temple. The deity commands that those who are engaged in these practices shall be purged. Ezekiel then sees his god mount his chariot and depart his temple and his city.

o   This divine departure answers the second exilic question: How is it that we were conquered if we are the covenantal partners of an all-powerful god? The answer is that the Jerusalem temple had become so polluted with foreign worship practices that it was no longer a suitable dwelling place for the Israelite god. Thus, like Ezekiel, this god must go into exile. When he vacates his temple and abandons the city of Jerusalem, he leaves it vulnerable to foreign attack and conquest.

Suggested Reading

Bloch-Smith, *Judahite Burial Practices and Beliefs about the Dead.*

Carr, *An Introduction to the Old Testament*, pp. 165–186.

Questions to Consider

1.   How do some of the behaviors exhibited by Ezekiel match up with what we associate today with the trauma of war and dislocation?

2.   What can we say about a Judean understanding of the afterlife based on Ezekiel's experiences and visions of death?

3.   Why is the mobility of the Israelite god important theologically for later Judaism and Christianity?

Life in Exile, Life in Judah
Lecture 17

In our last lecture, Ezekiel was our informant on the experience of conquest, deportation, and exile. We saw that his experience served as a catalyst for reformulating Judean theology, as the prophet imagined the Israelite god mounting a chariot and joining the exiles in Babylonia. In this lecture and the next two, we will continue to look at specific aspects of the exilic experience. In this lecture, we'll consider those Israelites who ended up in Egypt instead of Babylonia and those who remained in Judah. In the following lecture, we'll look at the issue of literacy and education in ancient Israel and Judah and the gradual development of monotheism as a religious belief system.

Multiple Experiences of Exile
- The biblical account of the Babylonian conquest of Judah would lead us to believe that nearly all the Judeans were either killed or carried into exile in Babylonia, leaving Judah a desolate and empty wasteland for three generations (e.g., 2 Kings 25:10–12).
  - In all reality, the total number of exiles taken to Babylonia was somewhere between one-fourth and one-third of the population.
  - The remaining three-fourths or two-thirds were killed in battle, fled to Egypt of their own accord, or stayed in the land of Judah.

- The segments of the Judean population were different from one another in several respects.
  - The Judean exiles who ended up in Babylonia were compelled militarily to leave their land. They arrived in Babylonia in three successive deportations, in 597, 586, and 582 B.C.E. These exiles were almost exclusively members of the upper class: royalty, priests, landowning nobles, and artisan craftsman.

○ In contrast, the exile to Egypt was, for the most part, voluntary. It occurred over generations as a gradual migration that began before the Babylonian period and continued after the Babylonian conquest of Jerusalem. Those who ended up in Egypt were mostly soldiers and traders—people of a lower class than those who went to Babylonia.

○ The remaining Judean contingent was most likely the majority. These were people who were not deemed important enough for deportation to Babylonia and had no reason to migrate to Egypt. They were farmers who knew how to eke out a living from the land.

Exilic Life in Babylonia

- During the first years of the Babylonian Exile, there were surely many Judeans who thought of nothing but returning home. Their anger toward their host country is expressed in the last lines of Psalm 137: "O Daughter Babylon, you devastator! Happy shall he be who requites you with what you have done to us! Happy shall he be who takes your little ones and dashes them against the rock!"

- With this mood of revenge in the air, a letter sent to the exiles by the prophet Jeremiah was probably not greeted with enthusiasm.
  ○ Jeremiah addressed his letter to a group he labeled "the elders" within the exilic community. The letter was sent early, after the first deportation of elites that included King Jehoiachin and the prophet Ezekiel.

  ○ Jeremiah's letter provides instructions from the god of Israel for the exiles to settle and continue raising families in the land and to pray for the welfare of their new home and those who inhabit it.

  ○ Jeremiah then predicts that the Judeans' time in exile will be 70 years. At the end of that time, the Israelite god will visit them once again and bring them back to Judah.

- We have few primary source materials that can tell us what life was like for the exiles in Babylonia. Instead, we find snippets of information that give us hints about exilic life.

  o The exiles were settled in villages near the city of Nippur along the Chebar River, an offshoot of the Euphrates. The names of these villages suggest that they may have been ruins of former cities.

Jeremiah's letter to the exiles proved accurate: They would put down roots in their new land for a period of 70 years before being rescued by the Israelite god.

  o Prophets who wrote during the exile described the exilic experience as a "yoke" they were forced to bear. When Jeremiah predicts the Israelite god's rescue of the exiles, his language evokes servitude: "I will break the yoke from off their neck, and I will burst their bonds, and strangers shall no more make servants of them" (Jer. 30:8).

  o Nebuchadrezzar's records list by name some of the Judean exiles from the first wave in 597. Significantly, these men included artisans and a gardener, people with skills that Babylonia could put to work.

  o Additional Babylonian records indicate that exiles as a whole, not the Judeans in particular, were used as forced labor in massive building projects.

- In addition to these details that suggest the difficulty of life in exile, there are other factors that point to the gradual adaptation of the Judeans to their new lives in Babylonia. Still other details point to an improvement in their living conditions, as we see in the story of King Jehoiachin.

o Nebuchadrezzar's records mention Jehoiachin by name and indicate that he and his five sons, along with other dignitaries deported from Jerusalem, received food rations. These records date to 592, just a few years after Jehoiachin was carried into exile.

o At some point in Jehoiachin's exile, he was imprisoned, but the final chapter of 2 Kings tells us that he was freed in the 37th year of his exile and given a seat higher than the seats of other foreign kings in Babylonia.

o His release from prison and restoration as the representative of his people may be seen as a positive omen for the Judean exiles as a whole.

• Other signs of adaptation extended to all the exiles, not just to the royal family. For example, during the years of exile, Aramaic, the lingua franca of the Babylonian Empire, replaced Hebrew as the Judeans' spoken language. Many born in exile could no longer understand Hebrew.

• The Babylonians allowed the exiled communities a significant degree of self-governance, and the Bible seems to indicate that in the absence of a monarchy, the exiles organized themselves into extended families, what the Bible calls "houses of the father."

• Despite this degree of adaptation and assimilation, the community of exiles managed to maintain its separate national identity. They maintained certain cultural practices, such as circumcision, the observance of kosher food regulations, and the observance of the Sabbath. Each of these practices was part of what defined life in Judah, but once they were practiced in Babylonia, they took on added significance.

Life in Judah

- Although the Bible suggests that the stay-at-home population was small and insignificant, several pieces of evidence point to a more robust presence left in Judah. Several Judean cities and villages, for example, show no evidence of destruction or a break in habitation during the time of exile. Apparently, these cities were not important enough to merit conquest or deportation.

- The book of Lamentations preserves the experience of trauma for those who remained in or near the ruins of Jerusalem in the immediate aftermath of the conquest (Lam. 2:10–11). Elsewhere in the Bible, those who remained in Judah are described as "the poorest of the land"; their purpose was to keep the vineyards, orchards, and fields producing in the absence of the landowners.

- Ezekiel contrasts the "whole house of Israel" (those who are in exile) with another group that he labels the "inhabitants of Jerusalem." From the perspective of this latter group, the exiles are those who are "far from the Lord"; thus, they claim that the land has been given to them (Ezek. 11:15).
  o Although Ezekiel was against this group in Judah that had claimed the land, Jeremiah saw land redistribution as part of the Babylonian imperial policy (Jer. 39:10).

  o Some of those who remained in the land during the Babylonian conquest may have seen their own economic situations improve.

- Beyond the years immediately following the conquest of Jerusalem, we have no written records to help us know how those in the land adjusted to the new situation. What we do know is that when the Judean exiles from Babylonia began to return to Judah in the late 6th century, they found an organized Judean population that had been offering sacrifices on the ruined temple mount during their absence.

Exiles in Egypt

- We have already met some of those Judeans who relocated to Egypt. For example, the prophet Jeremiah remained in Judah following the first and second waves of deportations. He then got caught up in infighting among those who remained in the land.

  o Ultimately, he and his scribe were taken by force into Egypt with a group of Judeans that had determined they would be safer there than in Judah.

  o In Jeremiah 44, we learn that the cities where Judeans ultimately settled in Egypt included Tahpanhes, Migdol, Memphis, and Pathros (Jer. 44:1). These were likely cities where some Judeans had already settled prior to the Babylonian conquest.

  o Those exiled to Egypt rejected Jeremiah's view that the conquest of Jerusalem occurred because Judeans were worshipping foreign gods. Instead, the exiles in Egypt insisted that as long as they had poured out libations and made cakes for the Queen of Heaven, everything had gone well. Once they stopped serving the Queen of Heaven, Jerusalem fell.

- After Jeremiah, we have a blackout period for the history of Judeans in Egypt; we don't learn anything more about them until a century later. In the 19th and 20th centuries, archaeologists excavated the Egyptian site of Elephantine and uncovered a Judean military colony that dates to the 5th century and later. Based on the written finds, the Judeans who lived in Elephantine had a temple to the Israelite god.

  o These exiles differed fundamentally from the Judeans in Babylonia, who developed their religious practices in the absence of a temple and a sacrificial cult. For them, the only legitimate temple would be one that was rebuilt in Jerusalem.

  o But the Judean inhabits of Elephantine had no problem erecting a temple to the Israelite god outside their homeland.

- Ezekiel, who lived in Babylonia, made the Israelite god mobile. The Judeans who remained in the land felt certain that their god had remained in Jerusalem, and they offered sacrifices to him on the ruins of the temple. The Judeans of Elephantine in Egypt built a temple in order to enjoy the benefits of a local manifestation of the Israelite god. All three segments of the fractured Judean population found new ways to access and worship the Israelite god.

Suggested Reading

Cogan, "Into Exile," in Coogan, ed., *The Oxford History of the Biblical World*, pp. 242–275.

Kessler, *The Social History of Ancient Israel*, pp. 118–127.

Middlemas, *The Templeless Age*.

Questions to Consider

1. What might our Bible look like if it had been compiled and edited by the Judeans who did not experience exile?

2. What is the significance of the Judean exiles in Egypt building a temple to Yahweh?

3. How does the immigrant experience in America help you imagine life for the Judean exiles in Babylonia?

Literacy and Education
Lecture 18

L iteracy did not begin in exile, nor was it limited to exile. But the fact that those deported to Babylonia included the literate—namely, scribes—meant that literacy became important for understanding life in the Babylonian Exile. In this lecture, we will look at the origins of writing in the ancient Near East and the growth in literacy that occurred during the monarchic period in ancient Israel. This broader history of writing will, in turn, help us to understand the subgroup of Judeans who ended up exiled to Babylonia.

Writing in the Bible
- When writing is portrayed in the Bible, it is consistently presented as a specialized and culturally valued activity.

- First and foremost, the Israelite god writes. And he writes important documents that are meant to have lasting influence.
  - Exodus 31 records the conclusion of Moses's meeting with God on the top of Mount Sinai, where he receives the two tablets of the law (Exod. 31:18). This is the central event of the Torah, and writing plays a crucial role.

  - The version of this same event found in Deuteronomy 5 describes Yahweh speaking to the whole assembly gathered at the mountain and then writing his words on "two tablets of stone" (Deut. 5:22).

  - One chapter later, God requires that the Israelites write his law "on the doorposts of your house and on your gates" (Deut. 6:9).

  - Deuteronomy was likely written in its earliest form during the 7th century; thus, this understanding of the divine word mediated through writing dates to the monarchic period in ancient Israel.

- When God called Abram to leave his homeland, he spoke; there were no written documents. Early prophets, such as Elijah, also heard God but did not receive any writing from him. However, in the monarchic period and even more so during the exilic and postexilic periods, God's words are delivered to his messengers in written form.
  - When Ezekiel is called to be a prophet and to speak out against the rebellious house of Judah, God delivers his orders on a written scroll and then commands Ezekiel to "eat this scroll, and go, speak to the house of Israel" (Ezek. 3:1).

  - A later prophet named Zechariah receives his message from the Israelite god in the form of a flying scroll that bears a curse for anyone who might swear falsely by God's name. Zechariah does not read the scroll; instead, God tells him what it says (Zech. 5:1–4).

  - In the book of Daniel, we find the reference that leads to the idiomatic expression "read the writing on the wall." In this story, the king (the son of Nebuchadrezzar of Babylon) holds a feast during which the royal family drinks wine out of vessels that have been looted from the Jerusalem temple. As they drink and feast, "the fingers of a man's hand appeared and wrote on the plaster of the wall." Daniel is summoned to read the words and predicts the end of the king's dynasty.

  - In each of these prophetic books, God's words reach his messengers not through a pronounced oracle but through the written word. Still, the written word in these cases is unintelligible to most.

Writing as a Royal, Priestly, and Imperial Activity
- As we traced the increase in bureaucracy in the time of the monarchy, one of the factors we noted was an increase in titled officials, including scribes and recorders; these roles point to writing as a royal activity.

o We also saw Jezebel write a letter and seal it with her husband's royal seal. This story presumes not only a literate queen but also a literate village noble or courier who could read the letter once it was delivered.

o During the siege of Jerusalem, King Hezekiah received a written letter from the Assyrian king's emissary telling him to surrender Jerusalem. Not only is Hezekiah said to read the letter, but he takes the letter to the temple and lays it out before the Israelite god, suggesting, again, that God could read it, as well.

o We also talked about Josiah discovering a book of the law in the temple and requiring the assistance of a prophetess named Huldah to read and interpret the book.

- In addition, the Bible presents writing as a priestly-prophetic activity. As we've seen, some prophets received the divine word in written form; further, writing was regularly associated with Israelite and Judean prophets and priests, including Jeremiah and Isaiah.

- Finally, writing was clearly an imperial activity. Egypt, Assyria, and Babylonia used letters and royal edicts to control their provinces. This required a network of bilingual, literate scribes and officials. Assyria and probably the Israelite monarchy used writing as a display of power, as well. Inscribed text on Assyrian victory steles and palace reliefs would have inspired awe, even if viewers could not read it.

The Question of Literacy
- When we talk about the issue of literacy in ancient Israel and Judah, we must ask ourselves how we determine what literacy is and how we define a literate culture.

- Based on the biblical stories, literacy was limited to an elite few: scribes, some officials, priests, and some royalty and nobles. We do not have any stories of commoners writing.

- Most scholars who study literacy in ancient Israel and Judah estimate that less than one percent of the population was literate. Within this tiny percent, however, we can also say that the number of literate people increased during the time of the monarchy.

- The archaeological record provides indirect evidence of literacy. Obviously, the discovery of a written document attests to a literate producer and assumes a literate recipient, but it's difficult to extrapolate from written documents the percentage of the population that was literate. We cannot even assume that the scribe who copied a document was able to read and understand it.

The Beginnings of Writing
- The earliest form of writing found in the ancient Near East is cuneiform. This script dates to the 3rd millennium B.C.E. in Mesopotamia.
    - In its earliest form, known as Sumerian, cuneiform was logographic, meaning that each sign signified a word. By the 2nd millennium, we see the introduction of phonetically based signs, in which each sign represented a syllable. This is the type of script associated with the language of Akkadian.

    - Thousands of cuneiform documents, mostly legal and economic texts, have been found incised on small clay or stone tablets.

- Egyptian hieroglyphics appeared around the same time as cuneiform. This means that Israel came into existence as a people and a nation in a region that had a long history of a literate elite.

- An alphabetic script was first introduced and used by the Canaanites as early as the beginning of the 2nd millennium.
    - The 22-letter Hebrew alphabet is a descendant of the early Canaanite alphabetic script. Such a script is easier to learn than a logographic writing system.

- The more accessible alphabetic script, however, does not necessarily indicate that more people in the ancient world became literate. A person needed a reason to become literate, and for those who remained part of the village economy, literacy had limited value.

- We have some evidence for writing before the monarchy. One of the earliest forms of written texts that archaeologists have uncovered is called an abecedary. The earliest abecedary dates to the 11th century and comes from the site called Izbet Sartah, which is near the Philistine territory. Other abecedaries have been found in villages, suggesting that a limited number of people were learning to write in isolated contexts.

- In the period in which the monarchies in Israel and Judah would have been more developed, we can document an increase in literacy through the number of inscriptions that are uncovered. We've already seen several of

The Gezer Calendar, dating to the 10th century, records a poem of sorts that divides the year agriculturally into periods of planting and harvesting.

these inscriptions, including the Tel Dan Stele (mid-9th century), Hebrew wall inscriptions and ostraca found at Kuntillet Ajrud, the Moabite Stone (late 9th century), and the Siloam tunnel inscriptions (late 8th century).

- Clay bullae that were used to seal documents written on papyrus help us understand the extent of written correspondence. In a building excavated in Jerusalem, archaeologists recovered more than 50 bullae dating to the period just prior to the Babylonian conquest.

- What the archaeological record as a whole demonstrates is the increased use of writing for recordkeeping and correspondence from the 9th through the 6th centuries B.C.E., the period of the divided monarchy. During this time, however, writing remained an activity of the elite, often directly associated with the monarchy and the temple. This is consistent with the biblical text that locates scribes and recorders in royal and temple settings.

Education in Ancient Israel

- When we think of education in the modern world, we immediately think of schools, and one of the primary goals of our educational system is to produce a literate population. The Bible, however, never once refers to a school.

   o The first reference to a school comes in a noncanonical book called the Wisdom of Jesus the Son of Sirach. This book dates to the 2nd century B.C.E.; in it, the author, who is a scribe, refers to a "house of instruction" or "house of inquiry." The context makes it clear that this "house" is an educational site (Sir. 51:23).

   o The existence of a scribal elite centered in the palace and temple suggests a training program of some sort. The office of the scribe may have been located in particular families and passed down from one generation to the next. This system makes a large scribal school unlikely during the time of the monarchy. Instead, the homes of scribes would serve as the sites of instruction for the next generation.

- Education in the Bible is not focused on writing. For example, the Book of Proverbs is a book of instruction—a set of teachings that a father passes down to his son—but it locates instruction within the family. It represents a curriculum of sorts for prudent and productive living, but this curriculum is home based and not dependent on writing. Many of the Proverbs would be memorized and passed down orally.

- Finally, the village family compound represents another site of education and training throughout Israel's history. Once again, this education would be family centered, skill focused, and not tied to literacy.

- Without question, writing became an increasingly important medium of communication throughout Israelite and Judean history, but the Bible never depicts writing as a universal value. Instead, writing remained a tool of the elite and was understood to be so powerful that it was the preferred medium of divine communication.

Suggested Reading

Carr, "Textuality and Education in Ancient Israel," in *Writing on the Tablet of the Heart*, pp. 111–173.

King and Stager, *Life in Biblical Israel*, pp. 300–318.

Toorn, *Scribal Culture and the Making of the Hebrew Bible*.

Questions to Consider

1. What does the Bible's association of writing with God, kings, and priests tell us about literacy in the ancient world?

2. What kind of education would a highland village child need, and would literacy be a part of it?

Religious Developments of the Exile
Lecture 19

When we think of the Bible today, we associate it with Christianity, Judaism, and Islam, known as the "religions of the book." They are also known as the three great monotheistic faiths. This last association has led many people to assume that the Bible reflects monotheism. And if the Bible is monotheistic, it should logically follow that ancient Israel, the culture that produced the Bible, was also monotheistic. In this lecture, we will define monotheism and examine its development in biblical writings. This topic is appropriate as our closing lecture for the exilic period because the clearest articulation of monotheism in the Bible occurs in the writings of an exilic prophet known as Second Isaiah.

Second Isaiah

- Second Isaiah begins his book with an announcement of the end of exile in Babylonia (Isa. 40:1–2). Jerusalem has served her term of punishment for the sins that resulted in conquest and exile; now that she has been pardoned, she can look forward to the return of her exiled children.

- In Isaiah 45, we learn the reason for the change in Jerusalem's fortunes. Cyrus, the king of Persia, has emerged as a force that may take down Babylonia (which occurred in 539 B.C.E.) and will inaugurate a new policy whereby exiled people are allowed to return to their homelands.
  - Isaiah sees Cyrus as the "anointed one" of the Israelite god (Isa. 45:1). In Hebrew, "anointed one" is *meshiah*, meaning "messiah."

  - Isaiah later quotes his god saying to Cyrus, "For the sake of my servant Jacob, and Israel my chosen, I call you by your name, I surname you, though you do not know me" (Isa. 45:4).

- o We then hear the Israelite god tell Cyrus who he is: "I am Yahweh, and there is no other; besides me, there is no god" (Isa. 45:5). This statement and several others like it in Second Isaiah are the closest articulation we get to monotheism in the Bible.

Polytheism in the Bible
- We have already seen several biblical and archaeological examples demonstrating that the Israelites and Judeans worshiped multiple gods. A few additional examples also suggest the polytheistic roots of ancient Israelite religion.

- The generic word for "god" in Hebrew is *elohim*. Whenever the word "god" appears in an English translation of the Bible, this Hebrew word is behind it. Interestingly, this term is plural. The singular form is El, which is the name of the high god in the Canaanite pantheon. When the Bible uses the plural form, Elohim, to designate the single Israelite god, it may reflect a history when Israelites and their precursors worshipped a plurality of gods.

- We see this plurality of the Israelite god through the concept of a "divine council," which appears in multiple texts.
    - o For example, in Genesis 1, we read of the creation of the world in six days followed by a day of rest. In this story, God's decision to create human beings is stated in the plural: "Let us make humankind in our own image, according to our likeness" (Gen. 1:26), suggesting that he is not alone in his heavenly dwelling.

    - o We find the same use of the plural in the commissioning of Isaiah in chapter 6 of that book. Here, the 8th-century prophet Isaiah stands in the temple and overhears a divine council meeting in which God inquires of other divine beings, "Whom shall I send, who will go for us?"

    - o The Book of Job opens with a very developed scene of a divine council, in which the Israelite god questions lower-level gods about the happenings in his domain (Job 1:6).

- In addition to the plural form Elohim that is used to designate God, we also have the personal name of the Israelite god that was revealed to Moses through the burning bush in Exodus 3. In his self-introduction, the Israelite god seems to explain himself and his relationship to previously worshipped divine beings.
  - The god who speaks to Moses through the burning bush first identifies himself as "the god of your father, the god of Abraham, the god of Isaac, and the god of Jacob" (Exod. 3:6).

  - In Exodus 6, the Israelite god again addresses Moses in a way that explains his complex identity. He says, "I am Yahweh. I appeared to Abraham, Isaac, and Jacob as God Almighty, but by my name, Yahweh, I did not make myself known."

  - This story of divine self-disclosure suggests that during the patriarchal period, Abraham, Isaac, and Jacob worshipped a kind of ancestor deity, the god of the fathers. It was not until the time of the Exodus that this god revealed his personal name and became the national god of the Israelites.

- In all these biblical texts that refer to the Israelite god with different terms and in settings that include other deities, we see separate strands of traditions in ancient Israelite religion. These strands suggest a complex history of worship practices and beliefs that gradually coalesced into a single national deity: a conflation of the sky god El; the ancestral gods of Abraham, Isaac, and Jacob; and a southern Sinai–related god named Yahweh.

Henotheism
- Henotheism is the worship of one god while conceding that others exist. An example can be found in the Ten Commandments: "I am Yahweh, your god … you shall have no other gods before me" (Exod. 20:2–3). This statement insists that there is a special relationship between Yahweh and the nation of Israel, but it seems aware of the fact that other nations have their own named national deities.

- Josiah's religious reform, enacted in the late 7th century, also insisted on the exclusive worship of the Israelite god and even went so far as to destroy the statues and cultic paraphernalia of other gods. But Josiah's reform does not say that only one god exists and all other gods are not gods. Instead, he calls on the Judeans to worship their national deity, Yahweh, exclusively.

Monotheism

- Psalm 82 has often been highlighted as a poem that captures a historical transition from henotheism to monotheism. This poem plays with the singular and plural forms of El and *elohim*.

  o The psalm shows knowledge of a time when multiple deities gathered to discuss the governance of the world. Each had his own portion to manage.

  o But at this meeting, the Israelite god accuses the other gods of failing to live up to their divine responsibilities, that is, of judging unjustly and showing partiality to the wicked.

  o So grave is their error that they will lose their divine status and become mortal; they will die like mortal men die rather than live eternally, as gods do.

  o With the demotion of the other nations' gods to non-god status, the Israelite god is elevated, and his new sphere of influence is the entire world.

- This returns us to the Babylonian Exile as the context for the first articulations of something that approaches monotheism.

  o When the Israelites and Judeans first experienced the empires of Assyria and Babylonia, at least some began to see the Israelite god acting on an international scale. The attacking Assyrian and Babylonian kings were viewed as nothing more than pawns in the hand of the Israelite god.

  o In other words, the experience of these massive empires contributed to expanding the Israelites' knowledge of the world. As the known world became larger, the sphere of influence for their national god also increased.

o   After conquest and deportation, this process of expanding one's worldview only accelerated. Ezekiel, as we've noted, responded to this geographic displacement by making the Israelite god mobile.

The Prophet of Monotheism
- Second Isaiah is known as the prophet of monotheism. He probably lived in Babylonia during the closing decades of the Babylonian Exile, and his writings introduce several new ideas concerning the Israelite god. Although the Israelite god had already begun to operate on an international scale in the writings of earlier prophets, Second Isaiah conceives of the Israelite god on a cosmic and universal scale.

- Another catalyst for change in the Judeans' religious beliefs was the up-close experience of Babylonian religious practices. Second Isaiah describes the Babylonians' process of making and worshipping idols (Isa. 44), and in his description, he shows himself to be an outsider to this culture, looking in with a good deal of disdain for what he sees.
  o   In many places in the Bible, the Israelites mock the gods of their enemies, but the tenor of that mocking generally concerns weakness on the part of an enemy's god.

  o   What's new in Second Isaiah is the description of the Babylonian gods as fakes. Because they are so clearly the work of human hands, Isaiah reasons, they cannot be divinities.

  o   In Isaiah 45:5, we read, "I am Yahweh, and there is no other, besides me there is no god." The suggestion here is that Yahweh is the only true god, all others are "no gods" or fakes, and the worship of these other gods is delusional.

○ This one god has anointed Cyrus of Persia to "let his people go." He uses the language of Exodus to announce a new rescue mission. The god of Israel, now understood in his full cosmic power, will rescue his people from Babylonia; he will gather them back to the homeland in Judah.

Evolutionary Scheme

- In this lecture, we've charted a neat evolutionary development of monotheism. It's important to note, however, that we cannot read the Bible as moving inexorably forward from primitive polytheism to civilized monotheism, nor can we place ourselves as the intended outcome of the biblical project. The Bible does not close with the book of Isaiah, nor does Isaiah represent the undisputed zenith in Israelite thinking.

- In fact, every articulation calling for the exclusive worship of the Israelite god or for monotheism in the Bible is polemical. The authors who put forward this view had to argue for it; their audience was resistant.

- In the Hellenisitic period, when Judaism and Christianity begin to emerge, polytheistic ideas were alive and well, especially in apocalyptic texts. Jews and Christians alike embraced a worldview that included Satan, armies of angels, and armies of demons.

- Thus, although something new does appear in the writings of Second Isaiah—the assertion that the Israelite god is the only living, breathing god who exercises power on a cosmic level—there is no evidence that all Judeans in Babylonia and, later, back in the homeland accepted and adopted a monotheistic worldview.

Suggested Reading

Becking et al., eds., *Only One God?*

Smith, *The Early History of God.*

Stavrakopoulou and Barton, eds., *Religious Diversity in Ancient Israel and Judah.*

1. How do the references to a "divine council" help us understand ancient Israelite theology? How did the Israelites picture their national god, and what was his sphere of influence?

2. What is the significance of ongoing polytheistic practices and beliefs in ancient Israel?

3. How do you think the Judeans' encounters with the Assyrian and Babylonian empires may have contributed to the development of monotheistic beliefs?

The New Israel—Resettling the Land
Lecture 20

In the exilic period, we watched Israel and then Judah navigate their way through two empires—Assyria and Babylonia—that sought and, ultimately, achieved control over the western states in the Levant. Cyrus, the king of Persia, reigned from 559 to 530 B.C.E. and conquered Babylonia in 539, ushering in what is known as the Persian period. This empire endured until 332 B.C.E. In this final unit of our course, we will look at many of the issues that became important in the resettled land of Judah, including conflicts between returning exiles and those who had remained in the land, food as a marker of Judean identity in the postexilic period, and interlocking issues of intermarriage, circumcision, and genealogy.

The Persian Period

- The Persian period in ancient Near Eastern history is known as the period of restoration and rebuilding in the biblical story. In this period when some of the exiles in Babylonia returned to Judah, two issues emerged in the context of rebuilding a community and the temple in Jerusalem.

  o The first issue is: Who belongs, or who is a Jew? The returning exiles encountered existing inhabitants of the land, and tensions over national and religious identity became central concerns.

  o The second issue concerns the elevation of the Mosaic Torah to the authoritative law of the land and the national charter for a reconstituted Judah.

- The sources we have for this period are numerous, but they are not clear on who returned when and how the rebuilding process unfolded. Still, it is possible to sketch a chronology of events and to identify key issues that Judeans faced after some of the Babylonian exiles returned to the land of Judah and found that it was not empty.

- The biblical sources include the two-volume historical work of Ezra-Nehemiah and the prophetic books of Haggai and Zechariah.

  - We also have Babylonian, Persian, and Greek sources for the period, although these do not focus on the tiny kingdom of Judah.

- The biblical sources describe the return of some of the Babylonian exiles to Judah under a Persian-sponsored policy of repatriation and rebuilding.
  - The book of Ezra announces this return by quoting an imperial decree. In the Bible, the quoted edict comes about not because Cyrus had any independent ideas or policymaking skills, but because the Israelite god had announced through his prophet Jeremiah that he would bring the exiles back and plant them once again in the land of Judah.

  - According to this edict, Cyrus understood his power over "all the kingdoms of the earth" to have come from the Israelite god, and it is Cyrus himself who wishes to rebuild God's temple in Jerusalem.

  - It seems highly unlikely that Cyrus credited the Israelite god with any of his success. Instead, it's likely that the Persian edict quoted in the book of Ezra is a Judean composition or rewrite.

- We do, however, have independent Persian evidence for the policy of repatriating conquered peoples and sponsoring the rebuilding of local shrines and temples.
  - The most important document in this regard is known as the Cyrus cylinder, a clay cylinder inscribed with cuneiform text in the Akkadian language of the Babylonians.

  - Although this text focuses on the Babylonians as the conquered people under Cyrus, the policies that Cyrus adopts parallel what the Bible associates with Persian imperial rule: Cyrus

The Cyrus cylinder is inscribed with cuneiform text in the Akkadian language of the Babylonians.

repatriated conquered people and sponsored the rebuilding of local temples, and he presented himself as the servant of the gods whose people he now controlled.

- The return to Jerusalem was not a one-time, massive transplantation of the entire exiled population. Instead, it appears that there were several waves of returning exiles that spanned more than 100 years of history. Further, a majority of those exiled chose to remain in Babylonia.

Issues in the New Israel

- The history known as Ezra-Nehemiah focuses on two major events: the rebuilding of the temple in Jerusalem and the establishment of the Torah as the law of the land. Although Ezra-Nehemiah privileges the viewpoint of those who returned from exile over those who had remained in Judah, we can nonetheless piece together several factions within this reconstituted Judah that did not agree on who should control the rebuilding of the temple or the law of the land. In short, they did not agree on who belonged in the "New Israel."

- The first act of those who returned to Judah from exile was to make offerings on the ruined mount of the former temple. After seven months, the returnees set about erecting an altar and laying the foundation for the new temple. In both of these events, we hear evidence of discord in the community.

- Those who returned from exile viewed themselves as the New Israel. They believed that they had earned this designation because they had endured the divine punishment of exile. This group had the advantage of imperial backing from Persia and financial support from the exilic community that remained in Babylonia. Ultimately, members of this group edited and shaped the Bible; Ezra-Nehemiah is written from their perspective.

- In the process of erecting the new altar and laying the new foundations, we meet several other groups of people.
  o The "people of the land" discouraged those who were rebuilding the temple and tried to frustrate their purpose.

  o Those called the "adversaries of Judah and Benjamin" (Ezra 4:1) may have been a segment of the Judean population that did not go into exile.

  o Another group that did not go into exile is said to have successfully sabotaged the rebuilding of the temple by sending a letter to the Persian authorities accusing those who had returned of sedition.

- There is even some evidence for divisions among those who had returned from Babylonia. There seems to have been a dispute over who would exercise authority in the newly rebuilt province of Yehud (Judah): the Davidic heir or the high priest. Ultimately, priestly authority would win out over royal.

- After several delays, the temple reached completion in around 520 B.C.E., almost 20 years after the first group had returned from Babylonia and erected an altar.

- The multiple waves of returning exiles clearly upset the balance of power that had existed in Judah for more than 50 years.
  - The "people of the land" were likely the Judeans who did not go into exile: the poor, the commoners, and the illiterate. They had made a life for themselves on the land, and in some cases, on the specific land plots that had once been the family inheritance of those who were in exile.

  - Those "Yahweh worshipers" that Ezra labels "opponents of Benjamin and Judah" could be Israelites from the north who had fled south to Judah to live.

  - There also would have been many foreign groups living in Judah and in territories that may at one time have been part of Judah.

  - The returnees themselves clearly represented a threat to those who were already in the land. And for the returnees, those in the land represented an obstacle to creating a purified, restored, temple-centered community worthy of the covenant with their god.

Intermarriage
- It is in the context of a reconstituted Judah that Ezra and Nehemiah raise the issue of intermarriage with foreigners.

- Ezra is described as coming from a priestly family and as "a scribe skilled in the law of Moses" (Ezra 7:6). He claims imperial authority to require the observance of the "law of the God of heaven," a law that is later clarified as the "law of Moses."
  - When Ezra arrives in Judah, probably around 458, he learns that "the holy race has mixed itself with the peoples of the lands" (Ezra 9:1–2). The "holy race" or "people of Israel" probably refers to the community of returnees, who had been back in Judah for about 50 years.

  - Ezra prays for this preserved remnant from exile, asking forgiveness for the sin of intermarrying with foreigners. The people then make a covenant with God, promising to "put away all these [foreign] wives and their children" (Ezra 10:3).

o   The book of Ezra closes with a decree that all returnees should put aside their foreign wives and remain separate from "the people of the land."

• Nehemiah served as governor of Judah during the same period as Ezra, and much of the material about intermarriage from the book of Ezra is repeated in the book of Nehemiah.

• Although it seems unlikely that the oath of all the Israelite men to put aside their foreign wives and their children was ever carried out on a large scale, the issue of intermarriage was clearly important to the community of returned exiles. They had managed to maintain their Judean identity as worshipers of the Israelite god while in Babylonia, but upon returning to Judah, they found that those who had stayed in the land did not share the same sense of national identity and boundary marking.

Public Reading of the Torah
• A second focal point for the restored and reconstituted Judean community is the temple and the Torah of Moses. In the books of Ezra-Nehemiah, the lengthy transition to a Torah-centered community is sacralized in a single remembered event.

• We learn that Ezra gathered all the people of Israel to Jerusalem in the seventh month. He stood on a raised wooden platform or pulpit, flanked by laity and Levites, and he opened "the book of the law of Moses which the Lord had given to Israel" (Neh. 8:1).

• Ezra then leads a kind of liturgy. He blesses the Lord, his god, and the people respond, "Amen, Amen," lifting up their hands, bowing their heads, and worshipping their god, whom they understand to be in some way present in this gathering around the Torah.

- While Ezra presents the Torah and reads from it, the Levites are described as "helping the people understand the law." We must remember that the Torah was in Hebrew, and many of the people gathered would no longer speak or understand Hebrew.

- During this Second Temple period, we begin to see several developments that will become foundational to early Judaism: the elevation of the Torah and the study of the Torah to a religious and community-forging ritual, the elevation of the role of scribes, and the elevation of the status of the Levites as translators of the law for the people.

Suggested Reading

Carr, *An Introduction to The Old Testament*, pp. 207–228.

Kessler, *The Social History of Ancient Israel*, pp. 128–157.

Questions to Consider

1. What factors contributed to internal divisions and debates in the Judean community during the time of the rebuilding of the temple?

2. Why might Persia have adopted a policy of repatriating exiles and sponsoring the rebuilding of local temples and shrines?

Food and the Family Meal—Boundaries
Lecture 21

F ood preparation and shared household meals were some of the most important activities that ancient Israelites engaged in throughout their history. Not only were these activities essential for survival, but they were also central to forging group identity and marking group hierarchies. In this lecture, we will first look at the diet of common ancient Israelite village dwellers and contrast it with the more sumptuous offerings of the wealthy elite. We will then discuss several descriptions of biblical meals that show how shared food preparation, service, and consumption could mark insider and outsider status, as well as internal group hierarchies. Finally, we'll consider food as an important marker of group identity in Judah during the Persian period.

Diet and Food Preparation

- The typical diet of an ancient villager included a good deal of vegetables and fruits. Some of the commonly mentioned plant foods in the Bible include figs, pomegranates, grapes, and olives. Carrots, cucumbers, and onions were eaten, as well.

- Grains and legumes could be eaten parched or boiled as a porridge in clay cooking pots over open-hearth fires. Several types of grains and legumes were grown in the region; wheat, barley, and lentils were the most common.

- Wheat was ground for bread, which was made daily. As we saw earlier, the women of the household would use a heavy grinding stone to grind grain into a coarse meal. Then the meal would be mixed with oil or water to make a dough, which was kneaded and baked.
  - o The widow of Zarephath describes the basic bread-making process. When she meets the prophet Elijah, she says that she has only "a handful of meal in a jar, and a little oil in a cruse," and she is gathering wood to make a fire and make bread for herself and her son (1 Kings 17:12).

o We have a slightly more detailed description of bread making in the story of the divine messengers who visit Abraham and Sarah in Genesis 18. In this story, both the ingredients ("choice flour") and the product ("cakes") are finer than what is described by the widow of Zarephath.

- Baking was done over hot stones in an open fire or hearth or in a domed clay oven fueled by wood kindling and animal dung.

- A common main course would be stews boiled with vegetables, legumes, and sometimes, meat. This would be served with bread to be used as a scoop for the stew and is still a common type of meal in Mediterranean societies.

- Fish would have been available to some. Biblical food laws allow anything with fins and scales to be eaten; all types of shellfish would be excluded. The discovery of fish bones at ancient inland sites indicates that fish were dried and salted for preservation.

- Available beverages included water, milk and yogurt drinks, and wine and beer. Grapes, pomegranates, and dates could all be fermented into wine, while barley could become beer.

- Meat was a rare luxury, eaten at festival meals and shared across large family groupings.
  o The value that ancient Israelites placed on meat is evident in the volume of religious legislation governing its consumption.

  o Meat consumption is almost always associated with a religious sacrifice and festival meal.

- Among elite families, there were added luxuries. For example, the Bible associates the rich with more regular consumption of meat. It is no accident that the two individuals that the Bible explicitly labels "fat" are a priest and a king, two classes of people that would have regular access to meat and a more luxurious diet generally.

- Ancient Israelites definitely valued meat for its protein and its taste, and the Israelite god required meat sacrifices. But the Israelite diet was largely vegetarian by necessity. Village farming life with limited herds would not allow for the regular consumption of meat, and a villager's daily tasks of mending terraces by hauling rocks, grinding flour, fetching water, and following after flocks would make any degree of heaviness the privilege of the rich.

Picturing a Meal

- The Bible makes frequent mention of gathering around a table or spreading a table with food; thus, it is likely that many families ate on a raised surface of some sort.

- Because the artistic record of ancient Israel is almost nonexistent, we do not have images of ancient Israelite feasts. We can, however, look to some of the surrounding cultures to get a sense of what mealtime might have looked like.
    - In the Assyrian palace reliefs, we find carved images of captives sharing a meal in their camps as they journey into exile. There, we see captives gathered around a single pot, probably a stew that is hanging over an open fire.

    - Another relief depicts the Assyrian king Ashurbanipal enjoying a meal in his garden. The king reclines on an ornately decorated couch and holds a bowl of wine, while the queen sits on an equally ornate throne, enjoying her wine. Between them is a table with carved animal-foot legs. The image closely matches a description of rich people in Amos 6.

- A villager's meal was likely somewhere between these two images of captives in a camp and a king in his garden. We can imagine a simple table, with family members sitting around it on woven mats on the ground and sharing a pot of stew and a basket of bread.

Food Consumption and Boundaries

- One of the things we learn from studying meals in the Bible is that the act of sharing food constitutes a group. Family members

The understanding that those who share bread are allies and owe loyalty to one another is also evident in the later New Testament story of the Last Supper.

reaffirmed their bonds to one another by sharing common food. Those who sat at the same table and shared bread were allies and friends.

- For two people to share bread and then one to turn against the other would be a cause for confusion and lament.
    o In Psalm 41, we read, "Even my bosom friend in whom I trusted, who ate of my bread, has lifted his heel against me" (Psalms 41:9).

    o The prophet Obadiah warns, "All your allies have deceived you; they have driven you to the border; your confederates have prevailed against you; those who ate your bread have set a trap for you—there is no understanding of it" (Obad. 7).

- An ideal family is one that eats and feasts together. We can trace this idea in the extreme ups and downs experienced by Job's family.
    o Job was "the greatest of all the men of the east" (Job 1:3). Part of the evidence of his greatness was that his sons and daughters would join together for regular feasts hosted in the houses of each of the sons in turn.

- o In this well-known biblical story, however, Job loses everything: his children, his wealth, his social status, and his physical health.

- o Once he has lost everything, Job complains of starvation. Instead of feasting with his family, worms are feasting on his decaying flesh. Rather than a family gathered around him, his wife is repulsed by his breath and his brothers loathe him. In the ancient world, to have no food, no family, and no shared mealtime with the family is to live the life of a cursed man.

- o In the closing chapters of the Book of Job, he and his family are restored. God returns his children, his wealth, and his health. Part of the vision of Job's restoration is the gathering of his brothers and sisters, who sit with him and once again eat his bread (Job 42:11).

- Food could also mark those who are outsiders to a group. One of the problems that the Bible has with Israelite men marrying foreign women is that these women will prepare outsider food for them. In Numbers 25, we see Israelite men eating food prepared by Moabite women, specifically, meat that had been sacrificed to a foreign god.

Elevating Status through Food Service

- Several meals described in the Bible show how food service could mark a person as special, as we see in the story of Joseph reuniting with his brothers in Egypt (Gen. 43). There, Benjamin receives a portion five times that of the others because he is the only brother with whom Joseph shares both father and mother.

- A similar use of food portioning to signal special status is used in the story of Saul becoming king (1 Sam. 9:23–24). In this story, Saul's status as a divinely appointed king is announced to a select group by placing him at the head of the table and serving him a reserved piece of the sacrificial meal.

- A man could also signal his love and devotion to his wife through the portioning of food at a sacrificial meal. Samuel's mother, Hannah, receives a certain portion at a sacrificial meal that is meant to communicate her husband's love, despite her lack of children at the time.

- In each of these meals, the male hosts seat the guests and determine the portions, and through the portioning of food, the hosts communicate the chosen and loved status of one of the recipients.

Dietary Laws and Maintenance of Identity
- One of the key ways in which food becomes a marker of identity is through the food laws known as *kashrut*, or kosher food regulations. The word "kosher" means "fit" or "appropriate."

- Dietary laws are found in Leviticus 11 and, with some slight changes, in Deuteronomy 14. In both cases, the food laws are couched in the language of "holiness."

- To be "holy" in the Bible means to be "set apart." Observing a kosher diet was designed to set the Israelite people apart from those around them. Observing the laws was also part of the covenant with God. In order to be part of God's holy household, the Israelites must keep his diet.

- The list of food regulations begins with meat. Again, because meat was a luxury, it is listed first.
  - The Israelites may eat any animal that has a cloven hoof and chews the cud, which includes oxen, sheep, goats, and several undomesticated animals. They may not eat pork; this restriction set them apart from the Philistines, Assyrians, and Babylonians.

  - Also forbidden are numerous flying creatures, although locusts, grasshoppers, and crickets are permitted.

- Trying to use logic or science to explain the particularities of these food laws has proven an elusive goal. The Bible does not provide any sort of logical or health-related justification for eating one animal and not another. Instead, we must go back to the statement: "Be holy for I am holy." These laws define the Israelites as a nation set apart and a people holy to their god.

Suggested Reading

Borowski, *Daily Life in Biblical Times*, pp. 63–73.

MacDonald, *Not Bread Alone*.

Questions to Consider

1. How does food serve as a boundary marker in ancient Israel?

2. Why might the kosher food laws have become more important once the Judeans were exiled to Babylonia and after they were resettled in Judah?

3. What role does meat play in the ancient Israelite diet?

National Identity—Intermarriage
Lecture 22

In our lecture on the return of the exiles to Judah, we noted that one of the most pressing issues for the resettled community was that of national and communal identity. This issue of identity is central not only to the compositions that were written during the exilic and postexilic periods but also in the stories of the Torah—stories written prior to exile but preserved and edited in light of the concerns of exile. In our final three lectures, we will focus on key concerns during the postexilic period in Judah. In this lecture, we'll look at the issue of intermarriage with foreigners by examining the remembered story of Dinah and the composed story of Ruth.

The Story of Dinah

- The story of Dinah, found in Genesis 34, is part of the Jacob cycle. This cycle of stories is considered one of the oldest compositions in the Bible, a set of stories that originated in the northern kingdom of Israel and focused on the eponymous ancestor of Israel, the patriarch Jacob.

- The story of Dinah occurs relatively late in the larger narrative about Jacob, who has already spent decades in Haran. He has four wives who have borne him eleven sons and one daughter, Dinah. He returns to his homeland in Canaan, to the city of Shechem.

- Dinah's story begins as follows: "Now Dinah, the daughter of Leah, whom she had borne to Jacob, went out to see the daughters of the land; and when Shechem, the son of Hamor, the Hivite, the prince of the land, saw her, he took her, and lay with her, and humbled her."
  - Several details in the wording of this story already stand out from the perspective of an exilic editing. First, Jacob, who is renamed Israel, has just returned from years in Mesopotamia. He has, in effect, endured his own exilic experience.

- Upon his return, his daughter goes out to meet the "daughters of the land." This phrase recalls the "people of the land" that the returning exiles encountered when they began to rebuild the temple.

- While out, Dinah is sexually violated by Shechem, the prince of the land, a Hivite.

- Shechem is drawn to Dinah and begs his father to negotiate his marriage to her.
  - Hamor, Shechem's father, begins negotiations with Jacob and his sons. Of course, the situation is not ideal because Shechem has already seized, abducted, and violated Dinah, and she is with him in his home.

  - The deal that Hamor puts forward, however, goes beyond a marriage between Dinah and Shechem (Gen. 34:9–10). He proposes a long-term treaty between the Israelites and the Shechemites that will involve an ongoing exchange of women in marriage. A postexilic reading of Hamor's proposal would view it as defying the Torah.

- Dinah's brothers ultimately agree to the marriage treaty for Dinah and, more broadly, for the two peoples, but we learn that the brothers had negotiated deceitfully. To allow intermarriage between these two peoples, Dinah's brothers demand that all the Shechemite men undergo circumcision. Several things stand out as strange in this request.
  - First, Hamor and Shechem are said to be pleased with this request and, without hesitation, have themselves circumcised. They have no trouble convincing all their Shechemite brethren to follow suit.

  - Second, the Shechemites were part of a larger group known as the Canaanites, and this group, as far as we know, practiced circumcision, perhaps as a rite performed before a man's marriage. If this is true, then it seems strange that all the

Shechemite men must be circumcised before one Shechemite man can marry Dinah.

- o Beginning in the Babylonian Exile, the practice of infant circumcision among Judeans became a cultural mark of identity, a ritual and sign that Judeans observed while in Babylonia, a land that did not practice circumcision. By the Second Temple period, circumcision was centrally important to an emerging Jewish identity.

- After all the Shechemite men had willingly submitted to circumcision, two of Jacob's sons, Simeon and Levi, "took their swords and came against the city unawares, and killed all the males" (Gen. 34:25).
  - o This mass slaughter of men who have just agreed to the terms of a treaty with Jacob's sons takes us by surprise even though the text indicated that the brothers had negotiated deceitfully.

  - o Again, what seems significant is that Levi in particular takes it upon himself to prevent a treaty of intermarriage with foreigners and that the dividing line between these two peoples is the practice of circumcision.

- The Jacob cycle is recognized as a pre-exilic composition; therefore, it represents one of the written sources that exilic editors incorporated into what ultimately became the Torah. It seems possible that the story of Dinah was shaped in ways that expressed exilic and postexilic anxieties around national identity. These anxieties found expression in the practice of circumcision, in the prohibition of intermarriage, and in the role of Levites interpreting and making sense of the Torah.
  - o This is what we mean when we say that the crisis of exile determined which stories were preserved and how they were told. Dinah's is a story that has a lesson for returning exiles, a message that the Levites were helping them understand: "Therefore, do not give your daughters to their sons, neither take their daughters for your sons" (Ezra 9:12).

- But as this lesson is taught in a brutal fashion, we also hear the anxiety and moral questioning of Jacob, who is, after all, "Israel." After Simeon and Levi have killed all the men of Shechem, Jacob laments that his sons have made him "odious to the inhabitants of the land" and vulnerable to attack (Gen. 34:30).

- Within this short narrative, we watch as Jacob, who is Israel, returns from exile and finds his daughter compromised by the "people of the land." He then sees his sons respond with violence, ostensibly over the issue of circumcision, and he worries for the survival of his household.

The Story of Ruth

- The book of Ruth was likely composed during or following the exile. It has a southern Judean, monarchic focus. In fact, the book closes with a genealogy of King David, identifying Ruth as his great-great-grandmother, and we know that during and after the exile, the figure of David received a tremendous amount of attention.
  - The book of Ruth may represent an attempt to deal with one problematic aspect of David's biography: He was a descendant of a Moabite woman.

  - Given this potentially damning family background, the book of Ruth seems to tell a story that at once acknowledges David's Moabite ancestry and presents it in its most positive light.

- The book begins by introducing an ideal family in difficult straits. The family is from Judah, representing the tribe that will produce royalty. But a famine in Judah requires the family to relocate to the land of Moab. Within three short verses, the father, Elimelech, and two sons are dead (Ruth 1:3–5). Elimelech dies first, and the two sons take Moabite wives, Ruth and Orpah. Then, the sons die, leaving the wife, Naomi, with two Moabite daughters-in-law.

- At this point, Naomi learns that the famine in Judah has eased; she decides to return to her homeland, but she tells her daughters-in-law not to come with her. She says that each should return to her mother's home, where she can have a new marriage negotiated. Orpah complies, but Ruth refuses, swearing a loyalty oath to Naomi (Ruth 1:16–17). The two return to Judah, arriving just at the beginning of the barley harvest.

- The first piece of information we receive once the two women arrive in Judah concerns a "kinsman of Naomi" on her husband's side, a wealthy man named Boaz (Ruth 2:1). Every detail in the description of Boaz suggests that he will rescue these women, who have no husbands to serve as their protectors. But it is the careful planning of Naomi and Ruth that results in a "rescue."

  o Ruth goes to the local fields to glean grain behind the reapers. Boaz learns from his reapers that this new arrival in the fields is "Ruth the Moabite who came back with Naomi." This identification emphasizes her foreignness.

© Dr Jorgen/Wikimedia Commons/Public Domain.

Israelite law stipulates that farmers must leave some grain for the poor to glean; in going to the fields, Ruth places herself in the role of "the poor."

  o Boaz then tells Ruth to glean only in his fields. He will ensure that she is not harmed by any young men and will provide water for her. When Ruth asks Boaz why he has treated her so generously given that she is a foreigner, Boaz tells her that he has heard of her kindness to Naomi.

- While Ruth took the lead in chapter 2 to secure grain for herself and Naomi, Naomi takes the lead in chapter 3 to arrange the marriage of Ruth to Boaz.
  - Naomi tells Ruth to wash and anoint herself and dress in her best clothes; she should then go down to the threshing floor, where the harvest festival will take place.

  - She is to wait until Boaz has finished eating and drinking. Once he falls asleep, Naomi instructs Ruth to "uncover his feet and lie down and he will tell you what to do" (Ruth 3:4).

  - When Boaz awakes to find Ruth lying at his feet, he realizes that he must either find her a husband or become her husband.

- The final chapter shifts the focus to Boaz and the men.
  - As in the case of Dinah, it is the men who negotiate who will get the land and the woman. The land is Elimelech's original land, and the two women are tied to that land.

  - Boaz calls a meeting of the town elders. At this meeting, he identifies one kinsman who is more closely related to Elimelech than Boaz. In the presence of the elders, he tells this kinsman that Naomi is prepared to sell her dead husband's parcel of land and that this relative is first in line to bid for it. The relative immediately jumps at the chance to add to his property.

  - But then Boaz informs the relative that if he acquires the land, he must also marry Ruth. This added information causes the relative to relinquish his claim, clearing the way for Boaz to take Ruth as a wife and to redeem the property of her dead husband.

- At the end of a book that has been about women's ingenuity in the face of famine and death, we have a restoration of the male-headed "house of the father" that serves as protection for the women. Ruth the Moabite remains a foreigner, but she is now deemed "more worthy [to Naomi] than seven sons," and her loyalty and industriousness have made her a worthy ancestress of King David.

Bellis, *Helpmates, Harlots, and Heroes*, pp. 57–83, 183–202.

Frymer-Kensky, *Reading the Women of the Bible*, pp. 179–198, 238–296.

Newsom, Ringe, and Lapsley, eds., *The Women's Bible Commentary*.

Questions to Consider

1. How does food figure in to the story of Ruth's ultimate acceptance into a Judean family?

2. Where do we find the voices of debate on intermarriage in the stories of Dinah and Ruth?

3. What qualities in women make them heroic in these stories? What qualities in men make them heroic?

National Identity—Twins and Enemies

Lecture 23

F ollowing the experiences of conquest, deportation, exile, return, and rebuilding, a central focus of Judean anger was Edom, a small kingdom east of Israel and Judah. Some of the exilic prophets composed oracles of judgment against Edom, simultaneously labeling it as cursed by the Israelite god and a twin of Jacob, Esau. In this association, we see Judeans working through their anger and sense of betrayal. Just as Dinah and Ruth became figures through which Israel renegotiated and debated the issues of intermarriage, Esau and the traditions surrounding him became the site for articulating Israel's chosenness and superiority over Edom, while acknowledging the close cultural and historical relationship between the two peoples.

Edom

- Edom was one of three small trans-Jordanian kingdoms east of Israel and Judah.
  - o During Judah's monarchy, Edom's territory began in the land southeast of the Dead Sea, while Judah occupied the land to the west of the Dead Sea.

  - o Over time, the territory of Edom moved westward to the southern flank of Judah; by the time of the Persian period, Edom became known as the Persian province of Idumea, and its territory included land west of the Dead Sea that had once been part of Judah.

- Again, thinking of our conceptual diagram of the composition and redaction of the Bible, some of the arrows moving forward from exile would include prophets composing oracles of judgment against Edom. These judgments simultaneously labeled Edom as cursed by the Israelite god and a twin of Jacob, Esau. Thus, if one of the questions posed by the exiles was "Who is the restored

Kingdom of Edom

Judah

Edom

Israel?" part of that answer would involve a clarification of Israel's and Judah's relationship with Edom.

Obadiah

- Obadiah is the shortest book in the Bible, just one chapter. Clearly, the author was writing in light of the conquest of Jerusalem, but it is difficult to determine how much historical distance he has from the events. He could be writing during or after the exilic experience.

- In many ways, this prophetic book fleshes out some of the details that explain why Edom was singled out for revenge in Psalm 137.

- While Psalm 137 calls on the Israelite god to "remember against Edom" concerning the event called "the day of Jerusalem," Obadiah narrates how the Israelite god does just that.
  o Several times in this prophetic book, Edom is made synonymous with Esau, Jacob's twin. We hear, for example, in

verses 9–10: "Esau will be cut off by slaughter for the violence done to your brother Jacob."

- o Then, in verses 11–14, we get a list of Edom's crimes that occurred on the day of Jerusalem's conquest by Babylonia, including standing aloof as strangers carried off Jerusalem's wealth, "gloating" and "rejoicing" over the ruin of Judah, and conspiring with the Babylonians to deliver up any Judeans who fled Jerusalem toward Edom.

- In verse 15, we shift from reading out the crimes to announcing the punishment.
  - o First, Mount Zion—Jerusalem—will be restored. It shall once again be holy. The house of Jacob will repossess what it lost to Babylonia and to Edom.

  - o And then we read, "The house of Jacob will be a fire and the house of Joseph a flame, and the house of Esau stubble." Given that Jerusalem had been destroyed by fire, Obadiah imagines poetic justice.

  - o Finally, Obadiah imagines the gathering of all the exiles from both Israel and Judah back to their homeland, where they will occupy an expanded territory that includes "the cities of the Negev," namely, the territory southwest of the Dead Sea that Edom occupied after the conquest.

- The short prophetic book of Obadiah narrates the troubled history between Judah and Edom. But throughout this historical reconstruction, Obadiah acknowledges Edom as "a brother" of Jacob. In some sense, it is this status as a twin that makes Edom's crime, according to Obadiah, all the more inexcusable.

Malachi
- Malachi is another short prophetic book by an author we know little about. His central message calls on the restored "Israel" to remain faithful to the covenant and its teachings. He likely wrote in the

5th century, after the Jerusalem temple had been rebuilt and the priesthood was once again functioning.

- In the beginning of the book, the patriarchal covenant is evoked; here, we find a reference to Esau as Edom.
  - The book begins with an oracle of the Lord: "I have loved you, says the Lord. But you say, 'How have you loved us?' 'Is not Esau Jacob's brother?' says the Lord. 'Yet I have loved Jacob, but I have hated Esau'" (Mal. 1:2–3).

  - This is already quite definitive as a statement of divine chosenness, but the oracle continues with a hypothetical question: "If Edom says, 'We are shattered but we will rebuild the ruins,' the Lord of hosts says, 'They may build, but I will tear down, until they are called the wicked country, the people with whom the Lord is angry forever.'"

- In both Obadiah and Malachi, we see Esau and the traditions surrounding him become the site for articulating Israel's chosenness and superiority over Edom.

Jacob and Esau in Israel's Stories of Origin

- Like the story of Dinah, the story of Esau is part of the larger Jacob cycle, a pre-exilic composition originating in the northern territory of Israel. Esau is a central figure in Jacob's story from conception through adulthood. What becomes significant about the preservation of this story in a postexilic Judah is the acknowledgement that Israel and Edom were as closely related as twins. Let's look at the story in its pre-exilic setting and then consider its postexilic reading.

- Jacob and Esau were the twin sons of Isaac and Rebekah. Like Sarah before her, Rebekah was initially barren, and only after Isaac prayed on her behalf was she able to conceive.
  - The story describes Rebekah's difficult pregnancy, but she then hears directly from God: "Two nations are in your womb, and two peoples, born of you, shall be divided; one shall be

stronger than the other, the elder shall serve the younger" (Gen. 25:23).

- o Significantly, the twins already represent two nations. Further, Esau is acknowledged as the older of the twins, and the Israelite god has chosen the younger.

- We learn that the firstborn "came forth red, all his body like a hairy mantle; so they called his name Esau" (Gen. 25:25). We then learn of Jacob's birth: "Afterward his brother came forth, and his hand had taken hold of Esau's heel; so his name was called Jacob" (Gen. 25:26). Both names represent plays on words. Esau's description marks him physically, and Jacob's marks his character; he is a usurper and a climber.

The story of Isaac on his deathbed reveals the power of the spoken word in the ancient world; once Isaac has pronounced the blessing on Jacob, he cannot take it back.

- The distinction between the twins also emerges in their life pursuits: Esau is a "skillful hunter, a man of the field," and Jacob is a "quiet man, dwelling in tents." Further, we learn that "Isaac loved Esau, because he ate of his game; but Rebekah loved Jacob" (Gen. 25:28). The parents each have their favorites, and not surprisingly, Rebekah's favorite is the younger twin, the one that God has told her will prevail over the older.

- In the adulthood of the twins, Jacob supplants Esau in three separate incidents.

  o He first tricks Esau out of his birthright, convincing him to trade the firstborn's portion of their father's estate for a bowl of lentil stew (Gen. 25). This story presents a caricature of the Edomites as descendants of a hairy, red hunter who is ruled by his stomach rather than his head.

  o The second act of supplanting takes place at the deathbed of their father, Isaac. Rebekah and Jacob conspire to have Isaac pronounce the blessing of the firstborn on Jacob rather than Esau (Gen. 27). Esau's fury is so great that he plans to kill Jacob, which is why Jacob must flee to Mesopotamia and spend decades of his adult life there.

  o In the third episode of supplanting, Jacob returns home to Canaan and goes out of his way to reconcile with his brother (Gen. 36). Gone now are the references to Esau's redness, his hairiness, and his stupidity. Instead, Esau is presented as a gracious and forgiving host who welcomes his brother home. By this time, Esau had become powerful and has taken up residence across the Jordan in the land that became known as Edom.

- Thus, the prediction that Rebekah heard when she was carrying these twins—"two nations are in your womb"—is born out in the return of Jacob as Israel and in Esau's move to Edom.

Preserving Jacob's Story
- If the returning exiles hated Edom, why did they preserve the story in this form? These stories recognize not only the humanity of Esau but the shared origins of Israel and Edom as twins. They also show Jacob reconciling with an Esau who is gracious, powerful, and giving.

- The story of twins captures a historical reality: that the Edomites and the Israelites originated as closely related peoples. We can document this close relationship in several ways.
  - First, the Edomites and Israelites shared a nearly identical language and had a similar kinship-based society.

  - Like early Israel, early Edom had settlements in the highlands that required terrace farming. Their early settlements consisted of unwalled villages. Their material culture was like that of early Israel, suggesting that the Edomites also survived on a combination of agriculture and herding in households that practiced subsistence living.

  - Even more significant, however, is the Bible's association of the Israelite god with the southern wilderness territory of Edom. In some of the Bible's earliest poetry (Deut. 33:2, Judg. 5:4), Yahweh is located in Seir, the poetic designation for Edom. Further, Deuteronomy 23 states that the Israelites "may not abhor any of the Edomites, because they are your king."

- All of this suggests that there was a long, interlocking history of Israel and Edom. The story of the twins captures their cultural closeness and may suggest that at one time, they were one people worshipping the same god, the god of Sinai, the god of Seir.

- The story of Jacob and Esau, however, also preserves the rivalry and tensions that characterized the relationship between these two neighboring kingdoms that competed for control over the southern Negev throughout the monarchic period.

- As was the case with the issue of intermarriage, we find multiple voices on the status of Edom. Late, postexilic prophets saw Edom as the cursed, the hated one of the Israelite god. Biblical redactors, in contrast, preserved a story of reconciliation between the twins, a story in which both men have matured and agreed to dwell amicably in their designated territories.

Mullen, *Ethnic Myths and Pentateuchal Foundations*.

Niditch, *My Brother Esau Is a Hairy Man*.

Questions to Consider

1. Why did Edom become such a hated enemy in the writings of the postexilic prophets?

2. What does the story of Jacob and Esau as twins tell us about the pre-exilic history of the nations of Israel and Edom?

Loss and Restoration—Two Biblical Stories
Lecture 24

A s we have learned, the Bible was compiled and preserved by a remnant of Judeans who saw themselves as the memory holders for "all Israel." On the one hand, it is a book written by and for a literate elite—the "winners" of this history. On the other hand, it is also a story of national loss—of land, family, sacred sites, and political and economic stability. It is the story of a displaced people who never fully regained a sense of home. Thus, in this closing lecture, we will look at two famous biblical stories of loss and recovery: Abraham's near sacrifice of his son Isaac and Job's loss of his children, his wealth, and his health.

The Binding of Isaac

- One of the first things that we learn about the patriarch Abraham is that his wife, Sarah, is barren. In the ancient world, children were considered a blessing from God, but they were also needed to assist in farming and household tasks and to care for their parents in old age.

- For these reasons, the miraculous birth of Isaac to an aging Sarah and Abraham was greeted with incredulity and joy. But in the story known as the Binding of Isaac (Gen. 22), God directs Abraham to take his son to the mountains and sacrifice him as a burnt offering. Only the intervention of an angel at the last moment causes Abraham to stop the sacrifice.

- This story evades a simple explanation or theological interpretation. In its ancient setting, it may echo known practices of child sacrifice, or it may teach the lesson of total obedience to one's god. If, however, we read this story from the perspective of the community that ultimately preserved it—those who had experienced conquest and exile—it takes on added levels of meaning.

o   First, the experience of barrenness and the fear of reaching old age without a child to care for one later would be acute after the trauma of war, when many young men were killed. The miraculous, divinely promised birth of a son to an older couple becomes a symbol of hope to a defeated population that had lost a generation to war.

o   Further, the cruel and inexplicable divine test to which Abraham is subjected is one perspective on what happened during the conquest. In other words, some of those who experienced exile undoubtedly saw it as a divine test, one to which they had to respond with total and unquestioning obedience.

o   Clearly, this story must be read on multiple levels. Isaac is the Judean nation—a nation that survives as a remnant and one that endures long enough to preserve a book in which the people reaffirm a covenant of blessing that includes multiple descendants, a great nation, and an eternal land grant.

The Story of Job

- The second story of loss and restoration is found in the Book of Job. There is still considerable debate about when to date the composition of this story, but whether it was written after the fall of Israel to Assyria or after the fall of Judah to Babylonia, it is clearly a story composed in the aftermath of a national catastrophe—in other words, probably in light of exile. Like the story of Abraham, the story of Job concerns the divine test of a righteous man.

- In the first scene of the book, God calls a divine council meeting and asks for reports from a group of lesser divinities, called "sons of gods." One of these lesser divinities is called "the satan," best translated as "the adversary."
  o   When God points out that Job is an "upright man," the satan suggests that this is only true because Job hopes that God will protect his blessed and wealthy lifestyle.

- o What follows is a wager proposed by the satan and accepted by God. God will remove Job's wealth, children, and health and see whether Job still blesses his god.

- o God agrees to the wager, and Job loses everything. But like Abraham before him, Job does not curse God. He remains upright and blesses God.

Structure of the Book of Job

- The stylistic shift in the Book of Job—from narrative to poetry and back to narrative—has caused scholars to consider the prose framework of the book as a unit related to, but distinct from, the poetic dialogues that make up the body of the book.

- If we follow this suggestion and jump from chapter 2 to 42, we find that in the first two chapters, Job does not curse God; he endures his losses and blesses God. Then, three friends arrive, having heard of Job's misfortune. They come to offer comfort, but when they see the devastated state of their friend, they can say nothing.

- Jumping to chapter 42, we find that Job's fortunes are restored and he lives to the age of 140. In this prose ending, Job passes the divine test. He shows that his piety is not self-interested, and as a reward, his wealth and children are restored.

- The prose narrative also provides an interesting answer to the exilic question: Why were the chosen people conquered? The answer, in this case, is that the conquest was the result of a divine wager that got out of hand. Like Abraham, the Job of the prose narrative is put to a test for seemingly no good reason. He endures an unspeakable loss, only to have it replaced at the end when he is deemed faithful.

- Both of these stories would hold meaning and hope for an exilic community in their acknowledgement of loss, their identification of God as in some way responsible for the loss, and the lesson they teach that those who remain faithful will experience a restoration.

- In some ways, the dialogue portion of the Book of Job is like listening in on an exilic debate about the extent of God's power, the nature of God's justice, the meaning of undeserved suffering, and the purpose of worship.

- Behind the question "Why do I suffer?" is Job's insistence that he is innocent of any wrongdoing; Job's answers to this question are unsettling.
  - He claims that he suffers because God is unjust. Either God has made a mistake and accidentally punished Job, or he's a tyrant and a sadist.

In the dialogue of Job and his friends, we listen in on a human debate over the nature of God, the extent of his power, and the meaning of suffering.

  - The friends' answers to the question of suffering are predictable but hardly satisfactory. They tell Job that he cannot be innocent.

- To the question "What should I do in response to this suffering?" Job's answer seems to be to interrogate God, demand justice, and fight for one's rights. His friends advise him to "make supplication to God."

- In their quest to understand this mysterious God, Job's friends consistently turn to the "wisdom of ancestors" (Job 8:8). Job, on the other hand, wants nothing more than an audience with the deity to argue for his innocence and against his unjust punishment.

Purpose of the Dialogues

- On one level, the Book of Job is about an individual who suffers and seeks to understand his losses in light of his belief in a just and all-powerful god. He finds the age-old answers to be insufficient.

- On another level, the experience of Job can be read as the collective experience of the Judean people, who lost everything through the experience of conquest.
  - o Although the prophets and priests suggested that the conquest of Israel and then Judah was the result of the people's sinfulness, the Book of Job seems to offer another explanation.

  - o The dialogues give voice to those in exile who might not accept the priestly and prophetic answer. These alternative voices ask: Is the punishment disproportionate to our sins? Why are those born in exile being punished for the sins of their parents? Is God just?

- The Book of Job as a whole challenges one of the central reasons put forth for the exile.
  - o We don't get a definitive answer about why people suffer or why nations are destroyed, but God tells Job's friends, "You have not spoken of me what is right." In other words, the supposed wisdom of the elders that the friends are passing down does not describe God.

  - o God then indicates that what Job has spoken is right. If we take this to mean Job's speeches as a whole, then we might argue that what Job did right was to question, challenge, and interrogate the tradition, even the part of the tradition that dared to describe the work of God.

The Restorations

- For many readers, the restoration at the end of the Book of Job seems hollow. Job gets no real answers. The same is true of the story of Abraham and Isaac. How do father and son have a relationship after the horror of Abraham lifting the knife over Isaac?

- Let's return to the question we asked at the beginning of this course: Who and what is biblical Israel?
    - As you recall, the first time we encounter Israel is in the story of Jacob. Here, Jacob must flee his brother and dwell in exile for two decades. Like the later exiles, Jacob put down roots and built a family and wealth.

    - Before he could return to the Promised Land and become "Israel," Jacob, too, had to pass a divine test. He wrestled with God, and like Job, he would not give up. He demanded a blessing, and God gave him a new name: Israel.

    - But at the end of this encounter, Jacob, now Israel, is wounded. Even in his restoration to the land and his receipt of a new name, he bears the permanent physical marker of a struggle with God.

- In many ways, the history of the ancient Israelite people parallels that of Jacob. They endured decades in exile and bore the yoke of the Babylonians. When they returned to their homeland, their restoration was both glorious and painful. They were permanently marked by their experience of loss.

- Like Job and his friends, the community that reassembled itself in Judah during the Persian Empire was fractured by debate. Like Abraham, Jacob, and Job, the Judeans realized that their restoration did not fully compensate for what they had lost. They looked at the rebuilt temple and wept over its former glory.

- The Bible as a historical library produced and preserved by this restored community in many ways heeds the advice of the Book of Job. It preserves multiple voices; it records debates; it allows its god to appear in multiple forms. It either fails or refuses to provide singular answers. Instead, it opens multiple entry points into the history of ancient Israel and its people, allowing the careful reader to catch glimpses of what life was like in biblical Israel.

Suggested Reading

Levenson, *The Death and Resurrection of the Beloved Son.*

Newsom, *The Book of Job.*

Questions to Consider

1. What can we learn about the Bible and the community that produced it from the dialogue of Job and his friends?

2. What kind of power does God have in the stories of Abraham and Job? How does he exercise this power?

3. What is the significance of the Bible's frequent reference to trauma-induced silences?

Ancient Near East/Fertile Crescent

Neo-Assyrian Empire

Bibliography

Ackerman, Susan. *Women and the Religion of Ancient Israel.* Anchor Yale Bible Reference Library. New Haven: Yale University Press, forthcoming. Due out in 2014, this book will bring together Ackerman's decades-long study of women's roles in the religion of ancient Israel.

————. *Warrior, Dancer, Seductress, Queen: Women in Judges and Biblical Israel.* New York: Doubleday, 1998. This book explores the roles of women in the book of Judges, including Deborah, Yael, the mother of Samson, and Delilah. For each woman's story, Ackerman brings in literature from the larger ancient Near East to help shed light on the possible interpretations of these women's social, sacral, and political roles.

————. "Household Religion, Family Religion and Women's Religion in Ancient Israel." In *Household and Family Religion in Antiquity,* edited by John Bodel and Saul M. Olyan, 125–158. Malden, MA: Blackwell Publishing, 2008. In this essay, Ackerman distinguishes between "household religion," defined as religion practiced within the physical space of the house, and "family religion," defined as religious practices engaged in by a family grouping in any site. She covers household shrines as described in the Bible and attested to archaeologically.

Bahat, Dan. *The Illustrated Atlas of Jerusalem.* New York: Simon and Schuster, 1990. This atlas traces the geography and architecture of the city of Jerusalem through archaeological excavations and biblical descriptions from the Bronze Age to the present. It has numerous maps and illustrations.

Becking, Bob, Meindert Dijkstra, Marjo C. A. Korpel, and Karel J. H. Vriezen. *Only One God? Monotheism in Ancient Israel and the Veneration of the Goddess Asherah.* Sheffield, UK/New York: Sheffield Academic Press, 2001. This collection of scholarly essays covers the archaeological and textual evidence for the worship of multiple gods and goddesses in ancient Israel and Judah while noting the articulated belief in "only one God." Of special interest to this course is the essay by Dijkstra on the inscriptions from Kuntillet Ajrud: "I have blessed you by YHWH of Samaria and his Asherah."

Bellis, Alice Ogden. *Helpmates, Harlots, and Heroes: Women's Stories in the Hebrew Bible.* 2nd ed. Louisville, KY: Westminster John Knox, 2007. In this book, Bellis not only provides her own reading and analysis of the stories of women in the Hebrew Bible, but she also brings together and synthesizes much of the existing feminist and womanist scholarship on these stories.

Bloch-Smith, Elizabeth. *Judahite Burial Practices and Beliefs about the Dead.* Sheffield, UK: JSOT Press, 1992. Bloch-Smith is an archaeologist who has documented various types of burial practices in ancient Judean sites. She examines the artifact assemblages found in Judean burial sites to determine beliefs about the dead.

Borowski, Oded. *Daily Life in Biblical Times.* Leiden, The Netherlands: Brill, 2003. Provides a concise overview of aspects of daily life, including hospitality, agriculture, warfare, life cycles, and the visual arts.

Brettler, Marc. *The Book of Judges.* London/New York: Routledge, 2002. Challenges the idea that the book of Judges can be used as a historical text providing information about premonarchic Israel. Although Brettler does not see a literary progression through the book of Judges, he identifies a pro-Judean orientation to the book that functions politically to prefigure the ascent of David to kingship.

Carr, David M. *An Introduction to the Old Testament: Sacred Texts and Imperial Contexts of the Hebrew Bible.* Malden, MA: Wiley Blackwell, 2010. This introduction takes an approach similar to the one adopted in this course, showing how Israel's encounters with the Assyrian and Babylonian empires shaped the history that is ultimately preserved in the Bible. Carr provides a highly readable and informative introduction to the Hebrew Bible.

———. *Writing on the Tablet of the Heart: Origins of Scripture and Literature.* Oxford/New York: Oxford University Press, 2005. Carr provides a comprehensive study of literacy and education in ancient Mesopotamia, Egypt, Greece, and Israel. He then examines the centrality of textuality within emergent Judaism from Qumran to rabbinic writings to the early church.

Chapman, Cynthia R. *The Gendered Language of Warfare in the Israelite-Assyrian Encounter.* Harvard Semitic Monographs 62. Winona Lake, IN: Eisenbrauns, 2004. Examines gendered language as the basis for historical comparison between Neo-Assyrian and biblical accounts of their shared military encounter. The book identifies and traces the historical presentation of royal and divine masculinity achieving victory over a feminized enemy.

Coogan, Michael D., ed. *The Oxford History of the Biblical World.* Oxford: Oxford University Press, 1998. This edited volume brings together some of the best scholars in the field of biblical studies to provide a series of articles covering the history of ancient Israel from the Late Bronze Age (1550–1200 B.C.E.) through the first Christian century (0–100 C.E.).

―――――. *The Old Testament: A Historical and Literary Introduction to the Hebrew Scriptures.* 2nd ed. Oxford: Oxford University Press, 2010. A detailed and highly readable introduction to the historical study of the Old Testament, this textbook would be ideal for people who would like to work their way through the Old Testament and gain an in-depth understanding of the history of ancient Israel.

―――――. *The Old Testament: A Very Short Introduction.* Oxford: Oxford University Press, 2008. A highly condensed version of Coogan's more detailed textbook (see above). In just 160 pages, Coogan provides an interesting and informative introduction to the Old Testament that would make an ideal reading guide for small Bible study groups that want to learn about the history of ancient Israel and the literature of the Bible.

Curtis, Adrian. *Oxford Bible Atlas.* 4th ed. Oxford: Oxford University Press, 2007. A good resource for understanding the land, climate, natural resources, and shifting historical boundaries of ancient Israel and the surrounding ancient Near East. Beautifully illustrated in color.

Dever, William G. *The Lives of Ordinary People in Ancient Israel: Where Archaeology and the Bible Intersect.* Grand Rapids, MI/Cambridge, UK: William B. Eerdmans, 2012. This book begins with an in-depth analysis of what archaeology alone can tell us about the lives of the people who lived in ancient Israel in the early 1st millennium B.C.E. His chapters on towns and villages, religion and the cult, and warfare are especially helpful.

Dever, William G., and Seymour Gitin, eds. *Symbiosis, Symbolism, and the Power of the Past: Canaan, Ancient Israel, and Their Neighbors from the Late Bronze Age through Roman Palaestina.* Winona Lake, IN: Eisenbrauns, 2003. This volume features a collection of scholarly articles on the economy, religion, and politics of ancient Israel and the surrounding nations. Of special interest for this course are articles by Lawrence Stager on the patrimonial kingdom of Solomon and by Susan Ackerman on worship of goddesses in ancient Israel.

Dutcher-Walls, Patricia, ed. *The Family in Life and in Death: The Family in Ancient Israel: Sociological and Archaeological Perspectives.* New York/London: T&T Clark, 2009. The essays in this volume examine family life in ancient Israel in light of archaeological data, such as house size and tomb assemblages, and bring these data into conversation with biblical texts reflecting family practices from birth to marriage to death and burial.

Ebeling, Jennie. *Women's Lives in Biblical Times.* New York: Continuum International Publishing, 2010. Ebeling is an archaeologist who has worked in both Israel and Jordan. In this book, she combines evidence from archaeology, biblical studies, and comparative literature from the ancient Near East to construct an imaginative account of the life of an ancient Israelite woman, whom she calls Orah.

Faust, Avraham. *The Archaeology of Israelite Society in Iron Age II.* Translated by Ruth Ludlum. Winona Lakes, IN: Eisenbrauns, 2012. An excellent introduction to the archaeology of the ancient Israelite village, household, material culture, social stratification, and political development. The book contains many helpful photographs, drawings, and charts.

————. *Israel's Ethnogenesis: Settlement, Interaction, Expansion and Resistance.* London/Oakville, CT: Equinox Publishing, 2006. Faust uses an anthropological approach to examine the emergence of ancient Israel as a distinct ethnicity. Some of the potential ethnic markers covered include meat consumption, circumcision, pottery, and house type.

Finkelstein, Israel, and Amihai Mazar. *The Quest for Historical Israel: Debating Archaeology and the History of Early Israel.* Atlanta: Society of Biblical Literature, 2007. This book is structured as a dialogue between two senior archaeologists who disagree about key aspects of ancient Israelite history, including where Israel first emerged as a fully developed state and the historicity of the united kingdom under David.

Fleming, Daniel E. *The Legacy of Israel in Judah's Bible: History, Politics, and the Reinscribing of Tradition.* New York: Cambridge University Press, 2012. Fleming unpacks the idea that the Bible we currently have is the cultural and political product of the single tribe of Judah, and within Judah's Bible, we find a select history of Israel preserved and reshaped according to Judah's self-understanding.

Frymer-Kensky, Tikva. *Reading the Women of the Bible: A New Interpretation of Their Stories.* New York: Schocken Books, 2004. A wonderfully fresh, literary reading of the stories of women in the Bible by an accomplished scholar of the Bible and the literature of the broader ancient Near East. Some of the women she covers are Rebekah, Sarah and Hagar, Dinah, and Ruth.

Hendel, Ronald. *Remembering Abraham: Culture, Memory, and History in the Hebrew Bible.* New York/Oxford: Oxford University Press, 2005. This book is first and foremost a wonderful read. Hendel takes his readers through the stories of Abraham, Exodus, and Solomon, and at each stage, he shows how memory shapes the narrative past while preserving aspects of history.

Kessler, Rainer. *The Social History of Ancient Israel: An Introduction.* Translated by Linda M. Maloney. Minneapolis: Fortress Press, 2008. Kessler provides a vivid portrait of the economic, social, and political realities of ancient Israel from a social science perspective. He covers topics ranging from ancient class societies and the development of ancient states to the endurance of kinship-based leadership structures.

King, Philip J., and Lawrence E. Stager. *Life in Biblical Israel*. Library of Ancient Israel. Louisville, KY/London: Westminster John Knox Press, 2001. An excellent introduction to daily life in ancient Israel, this book provides wonderful, detailed treatments of family, food, healing, music, travel, and much more. This is also one of the best resources for outstanding color photos and illustrations of daily life.

Levenson, Jon. *The Death and Resurrection of the Beloved Son: The Transformation of Child Sacrifice in Judaism and Christianity*. New Haven: Yale University Press, 1993. Traces the historical development of ideas concerning child sacrifice from Canaanite and early Israelite practices through early Christianity. Some of the stories covered include Abraham's near sacrifice of Isaac, Hagar's exposure of the child Ishmael, and the crucifixion of Jesus understood as a divine sacrifice of the beloved son.

MacDonald, Nathan. *Not Bread Alone: The Uses of Food in the Old Testament*. New York: Oxford University Press, 2008. MacDonald examines the diet of the ancient Israelites in successive historical periods: pre-state Israel, monarchic Israel, and the postexilic period. In each period, he shows how food and the symbolism associated with food intersected with cultural memory, religious and social judgment at the table, and ethnic identity.

Machinist, Peter. "The Rab Sāqêh at the Wall of Jerusalem: Israelite Identity in the Face of the Assyrian 'Other.'" *Hebrew Studies* 41 (2000): 155–168. This article provides a careful historical analysis of Assyrian and biblical texts that cover Sennacherib's siege of Jerusalem in 701 B.C.E. Machinist identifies several historical voices within the biblical narrative account of the siege through which Israel seeks to understand itself in relationship to a foreign conqueror.

———. "The Fall of Assyria in Comparative Ancient Perspective." In *Assyria 1995*, edited by Simo Parpola and Robert M. Whiting, 179–195. Helsinki: Helsinki University Press, 1997. Bringing together the written records of Assyria, Babylonia, and ancient Israel, Machinist examines the evidence for how and why the Assyrian Empire ultimately fell.

Mazar, Amihai. *Archaeology of the Land of the Bible*, Vol. 1: *10,000–586 B.C.E.* The Anchor Yale Bible Reference Library. New Haven, CT: Yale University Press, 1992. A comprehensive overview of archaeological sites and artifacts from ancient Israel.

McCarter, P. Kyle. *Ancient Inscriptions: Voices from the Biblical World.* Washington DC: Biblical Archaeology Society, 1996. Provides a history of writing in the ancient Near East, from cuneiform to hieroglyphics through the development of an alphabetic text and the emergence of Hebrew as a distinct language and script.

Meyers, Carol, Toni Craven, and Ross S. Kramer, eds. *Women in Scripture: A Dictionary of Named and Unnamed Women in the Hebrew Bible, the Apocryphal/Deuterocanonical Books, and the New Testament.* Grand Rapids, MI/Cambridge, UK: William B. Eerdmans, 2000. An excellent go-to resource for identifying and understanding all the women characters mentioned in the Bible. There are entries for the Queen of Heaven and Jephthah's daughter, as well as the better known women, such as Sarah, Rebekah, and Rachel.

Meyers, Carol. *Rediscovering Eve: Ancient Israelite Women in Context.* New York: Oxford University Press, 2013. Meyers draws on decades of archaeological research and biblical study to provide a detailed portrait of the life of average ancient Israelite women. She demonstrates women's essential roles in the household, the village economy, the religious sphere, and public life.

Middlemas, Jill. *The Templeless Age: An Introduction to the History, Literature, and Theology of the Exile.* Louisville, KY: Westminster John Knox, 2007. In her study of ancient Judah during the period of the Babylonian Exile, Middlemas emphasizes the importance of the group of Judeans who remained in the land and did not experience exile. Her title, *The Templeless Age*, is meant as a corrective to those scholars who follow the Bible's own bias for the exilic community.

Mieroop, Marc Van De. *A History of the Ancient Near East, ca. 3000–323 BC*. Blackwell History of the Ancient World. Malden, MA: Blackwell Publishing, 2004. This book provides a fascinating treatment of the history of the ancient Near East. Part III on empires is especially informative in illuminating the Assyrian, Babylonian, and Persian empires, which heavily influenced the history of ancient Israel.

Mullen, E. Theodore Jr. *Ethnic Myths and Pentateuchal Foundations: A New Approach to the Formation of the Pentateuch*. Atlanta: Scholars Press, 1997. This book argues for a late Persian period dating for the composition of the Pentateuch based on what Mullen describes as a fully developed narrative of ethnic and national identity.

Newsom, Carol A., Sharon H. Ringe, and Jacqueline E. Lapsley, eds. *The Women's Bible Commentary*. 3rd ed. Louisville, KY: Westminster John Knox, 2012. This newly compiled biblical commentary represents an outstanding collection of essays on every book of the Old and New Testaments and the Apocrypha written by some of the best scholars in the field of biblical studies. Additional essays cover issues or such figures as Hagar, Miriam, and Job's wife.

Newsom, Carol A. *The Book of Job: A Contest of Moral Imaginations*. Oxford: Oxford University Press, 2003. A theoretically sophisticated yet highly readable treatment of the moral and religious complexities of the Book of Job. Like the Book of Job itself, Newsom refrains from providing a singular interpretation and instead advocates a multidimensional or "polyphonic" reading.

Niditch, Susan. *My Brother Esau Is a Hairy Man: Hair and Identity in Ancient Israel*. New York: Oxford University Press, 2008. In this book, Niditch explores hair as a marker of identity in biblical narratives and shows how hair contributes to perceptions of social status, sacredness, and gender. Stories covered include Jacob and Esau, as well as Samson and Delilah.

———. *Oral World and Written Word: Ancient Israelite Literature*. Louisville, KY: Westminster John Knox, 1996. In this book, Niditch identifies an oral-written continuum in the preservation of ancient Israelite culture. Written in a highly accessible style, this book is an excellent introduction to the shared roles of orality and literacy in the formation of the Hebrew Bible.

Oberlin College Special Collections. *H. G. May Archaeology of Palestine Collection.* http://www2.oberlin.edu/library/special/religion/may.html (open-source archive). Several of the archaeological artifacts shown in the video version of this course are part of the Herbert G. May teaching collection at Oberlin College. Professor May was an internationally recognized linguist, cartographer, biblical translator, and theologian. Between 1934 and 1966, he was a professor of Old Testament Language and Literature at the Oberlin Graduate School of Theology. May was an avid photographer, and the Oberlin College library has recently digitized his collection of more than 3,000 lanternslides taken in British Mandate Palestine from the 1930s and 1940s and into the period of the State of Israel, from the 1940s to the 1960s. Images include archaeological dig sites and scenes in the daily life of villagers and city dwellers in Palestine during the mid-20th century. Many of the black-and-white slides were hand tinted by May's wife, Helen.

Oxford University Press. *Oxford Biblical Studies Online.* http://www. oxfordbiblicalstudies.com/Public/Home.html?url=%2Fapp%3Fservice%3 Dexternalpagemethod%26method%3Dview%26page%3DHome&failReas on=. A valuable online resource for biblical research and study.

Perdue, Leo G., Joseph Blenkinsopp, John J. Collins, and Carol Meyers. *Families in Ancient Israel.* Louisville, KY: Westminster John Knox, 1997. In five chronologically organized chapters, this book examines the family in ancient Israel from the premonarchic period (1200–1000 B.C.E.) through the Persian and Hellenistic periods (100 B.C.E.).

Rainey, Anson F., and R. Steven Notley. *The Sacred Bridge: Carta's Atlas of the Biblical World.* Jerusalem: Carta, 2006. An oversized volume with beautiful color maps, photographs, and charts that take the reader through the geography and history of ancient Israel and the ancient Near East from the Calcolithic Age to the time of the Bar Kokhba Revolt (3500 B.C.E.–130 C.E.). Concise articles accompany each period of ancient history.

Schmid, Konrad. *The Old Testament: A Literary History.* Translated by Linda M. Maloney. Minneapolis, MN: Fortress Press, 2012. This book challenges the traditional documentary hypothesis that divides the Pentateuch into four discrete sources. Schmid provides a new synthesis of European and American scholarship on the formation of the Hebrew canon.

Smith, Mark. S. *The Early History of God: Yahweh and the Other Deities in Ancient Israel.* Grand Rapids, MI: William B. Eerdmans, 2002. Documents and analyzes the diversity of ancient Israel's religious practices and beliefs. Tracing the development of Israelite monotheism, Smith shows the early connections between Yahweh and Ba'al, Asherah, and the sun god.

———. *The Memoirs of God.* Minneapolis, MN: Fortress Press, 2004. Smith approaches the Bible as the historical memories of a people and finds within those memories a development of thinking about "structures of divinity" that ultimately led to an articulation of biblical monotheism.

Stavrakopoulou, Francesca, and John Barton, eds. *Religious Diversity in Ancient Israel and Judah.* New York: T&T Clark, 2010. This volume covers the tremendous diversity in religious practices and beliefs in ancient Israel and Judah, including views of the afterlife, ancient Israel's absorption of aspects of Canaanite religion, and distinctions in religious practices between rural and urban, royal and local, north and south.

Steinberg, Naomi. *Kinship and Marriage in Genesis: A Household Economics Perspective.* Minneapolis, MN: Fortress Press, 1993. Provides an excellent treatment of the types of marriages depicted in Genesis and the economic implications of monogamy and various forms of plural marriage.

Toorn, Karel van der. *Scribal Culture and the Making of the Hebrew Bible.* Cambridge, MA/London: Harvard University Press, 2007. Van der Toorn provides an outstanding and detailed examination of writing and scribal practice in the formation of the Hebrew canon.

Ussishkin, David. *The Conquest of Lachish by Sennacherib.* Tel Aviv: Institute of Archaeology, Tel Aviv University, 1982. This is the definitive study of Sennacherib's defeat of Lachish, taking into account the archaeology of the site, the Assyrian palace reliefs and royal inscriptions, and the biblical account.

Bibliography

Notes

Notes